A
Pattern of
Hundreds

A Pattern of Hundreds

compiled by Members of
The Buckinghamshire Federation
of Women's Institutes

FOREWORD BY
SIR JOHN BETJEMAN

illustrated by
Trevor Newton

published by
Richard Sadler Ltd
for
The Buckinghamshire Federation of Women's Institutes

First published 1975 by Richard Sadler Ltd ,
Halfpenny Furze, Mill Lane, Chalfont St Giles,
Buckinghamshire

Printed by: Garden City Press Ltd, Letchworth, Herts.

Foreword

What is local is what is best. Old people's memories often tell you more even than old photographs. That is why I welcome this record in prose, some as lyrical as a poem, of the Bucks that is now only a memory.

I have known Buckinghamshire for sixty years, venturing out first as a child of nine or ten by Metropolitan from Baker Street but remember getting as far as Verney Junction. As an Oxford undergraduate I went by steam train to Olney to see Cowper's house and museum. I taught at Thorpe House, Oval Way, Gerrards Cross when aged nineteen or maybe twenty. The headmaster and his wife, Mr and Mrs Noble, used to take out my fellow assistant master and me, by open car through lime-scented lanes in the summer evenings. We were always pleased when we got back in time to race down to Chalfont St. Peter to buy half a pint of beer.

My most romantic memory of Bucks was seeing the Brill train with steam up waiting at Wood Siding Halt, the least known, remotest and quietest station on the Metropolitan.

Memories far more varied and vivid than these, are in the pages of this book.

London
April, 1975

John Betjeman

Contents

I
Ashendon
Hundred

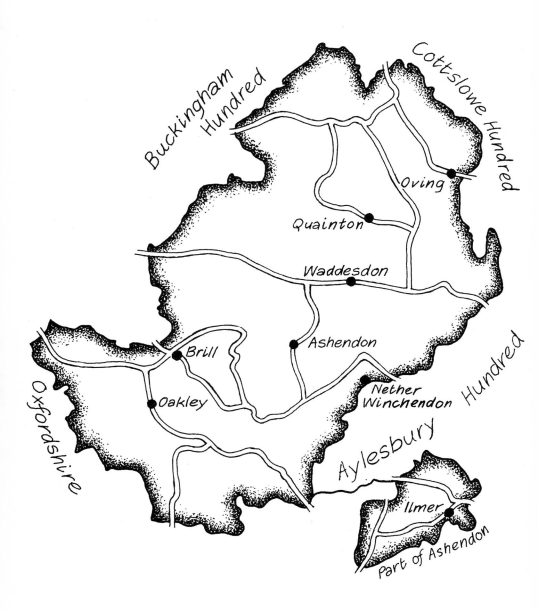

Buckingham Hundred

Cottslowe Hundred

Oving

Quainton

Waddesdon

Ashendon

Brill

Oakley

Nether
Winchendon

Aylesbury Hundred

Oxfordshire

Ilmer

Part of Ashendon

Until just before the First World War, Ashendon was a completely agricultural village. About that time, the first farmworker broke away from that way of life to work on the railway, and this caused a stir.

There were and still are seven farms in Ashendon with eight to ten men working on each. Farm workers were very proud of the farms they worked on and there was a friendly rivalry between them. It used to be customary for the men to meet in the evenings to compare the day's happenings and to boast of their achievements. They had great pride in their work.

Farmers brewed their own beer in large quantities as it was part of the men's wages. They had beer mid-morning, beer with their lunch and beer at tea-time. The more they had the better they worked. The mower had a pint at 4 am before starting work. Probably a hundred gallons of beer was drunk by each man a year. At haymaking they had a pint between each load and at night there was free access to the cellar. Despite this they were always fit and ready for work the next morning.

As in most villages, there was the annual Feast which was the great event of the year. It usually took the form of sports with a good feed afterwards and was always held on the first Tuesday in May. The farmworkers were given the day off as a paid holiday for this occasion. They usually took the next day off as well, to recover.

Molly Boughton, *Ashendon*

3

Fred Orchard of Nether Winchendon, now in his eighties, remembers how the postman walked from Waddesdon, starting at six o'clock in the morning and visiting all the farms on his way, thus considerably lengthening the journey of five miles. After a break for lunch, he walked on to Cuddington to meet the pony cart bringing the mail, then back to Winchendon to clear the box at about four o'clock and back to Waddesdon, often in the winter in thick snow which seems to have fallen more frequently in those days.

The village people, with wooden yokes on their shoulders and two buckets, fetched all water from a conduit in the Manor farmyard, or for those on the hill, from a spring half way down. Fred recalls this was his first duty after school, both for his mother and a bedridden neighbour.

There were fifty to sixty children of all ages in the little school, the infants ranged in rows on a gallery. In Upper Winchendon the Rothschilds dressed the girls in red cloaks and round straw hats, and the boys in white jackets, belted and reaching nearly to the knees, and a peaked cap.

The lady living at the Manor Farm started the brass band which later joined with Cuddington to form the Robin Hood Band, so called because Lt. Col. Francis Bernard and Mrs Bernard of Nether Winchendon House provided them with uniforms of Lincoln green—thick green coat and green trousers with a red bib, which later was changed to red collar and cuffs, and a soft felt hat with a feather at one side. They used to play for two days after Christmas, and also at Club feasts and at the flower shows which were held in large tents in a field, and there was great rivalry among the four villages—Nether Winchendon, Cuddington, Chearsley and Gibraltar. The wives of the bandsmen always sent an Aylesbury duck, dressed and trussed for the table.

Bertha Orchard remembers how in the 1914 war

the children were given a holiday to pick blackberries which were weighed at school and then sent to make jam. They also gathered horse-chestnuts which were taken to a local farm to be ground down for cattle feed.

Mr Welford's carrier cart took people to Aylesbury but the journey was so slow that by the time you got there it was nearly time to come home again!

C. Archer, *Cuddington*

I was born in 1892 a few years after the completion of Waddesdon Manor by Baron Ferdinand de Rothschild. Many houses were built in Waddesdon village to house the estate workers. Some of the older villagers can still remember the special railway built to transport the stone up the hill for the building of the Manor, and the teams of imported French Percheron horses which pulled the trailers loaded with fully grown trees selected from mature estates elsewhere, to be replanted in Waddesdon grounds. Waddesdon Manor has always been referred to by local people as 'The Mansion.'

The village flourished under the wing of the Rothschild family who did so much for everyone.

Waddesdon

5

Once a year in the summer was the Baron's treat, when all were invited into the Manor grounds where a band played and tea was served in marquees. People would come from the surrounding district in their pony and traps.

Each year at school prize-giving, the best senior pupils would be presented with a gift. The boys had a box writing-desk, and the girls had work boxes. These articles are still treasured in many Waddesdon homes by the descendants of those lucky children.

It was always known when important visitors were to come to Waddesdon and the children would walk to the crossroads where the main entrance used to be, to see such personages as Queen Victoria, or Mr Gladstone arrive. When King George V and Queen Mary came, they made their exit through the village, and drove very slowly for the benefit of the local people.

The village feast, at which roundabouts and swings were popular, was held at Michaelmas on the village green, a site now occupied by the Fire Station. Another excitement was the visit of the Wild Beast Show. There were cages of wild animals, and one year large crowds were attracted when it was advertised that Freddy West, the local barber, would enter the lions' cage, which he did with white face and trembly knees.

The first cars to come through Waddesdon came at walking pace preceded by a man with a red flag. Then came the first bus, called the Waddesdon Queen. Besides being used for journeys to Aylesbury the bus could be hired and was used to take a party to the Wembley Exhibition. Later Mr Cherry ran a bus called Cherry Blossom which was popular because it ran several times a day.

Daisy Adams, Daphne Campbell, *Waddesdon*

I I
Aylesbury
Hundred

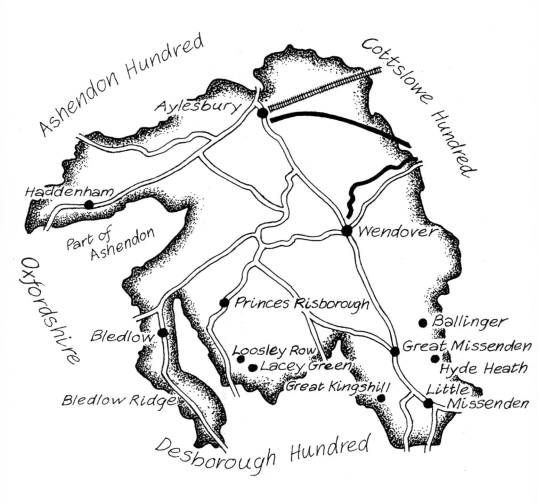

Ashendon Hundred

Cottslowe Hundred

Aylesbury

Haddenham

Part of Ashendon

Oxfordshire

Wendover

Bledlow

Princes Risborough

Ballinger

Great Missenden

Loosley Row
Lacey Green

Hyde Heath

Bledlow Ridge

Great Kingshill

Little Missenden

Desborough Hundred

'A lot of the cottages in the village were the foster homes for Dr Barnardo's children. Widows were often better off than the wives of the farmworkers because they fostered several children at once and had more housekeeping money.'

'I remember the women sitting in a circle doing their straw plait. The stone floors of the cottage were so cold that a bucket full of hot ashes were passed round under the women's skirts to keep them warm. Once one of the toddlers burned himself badly when he fell on the bucket.'

'Little Billy was a bit simple. It was said his mother gave him an overdose of laudanum when she was doing the straw plait and he slept for two days.'

'For lunch on Saturday we used to have a huge muffin covered with chopped vegetables and tomatoes.'

'Bird pie and rabbit was often eaten for the meat dish. The birds were trapped with a net as they flew from the hedges and from the ivy growing on the houses.'

'When roads need mending, the Overseer of the Parish had to find which farmers owned nearby land with plenty of flints, known as 'Buckinghamshire Diamonds'. In this area of the Chilterns, the Overseers were the Parish Wardens. The farmers were told how many 'yards' of flints were needed and if necessary, they had to employ the labour to pick up the stones to meet demand. It was the Overseer's job to find someone with a horse and cart to collect the piles of stones. It was a fairly amicable 'gentleman's agreement' type of arrangement and a good Overseer spread the load fairly round the local farmers.

'Boys were paid sixpence for picking up a 'yard' of stones, which was measured with a yard-square wooden box without a bottom. When full, the measure was simply picked up, leaving a pile of flints on the field.'

'I can remember the bodgers' tents with the lathe for turning chair legs. My father walked to Hampden to work in the woods.'

'There were brick fields at Sly Corner; clay was dug out of local gardens for bricks.'

'The beginning of May was Wendover Fair. The end of May there was the tea meeting at the Baptist Chapel. Mid July there was the Great Missenden Benefit Club Entertainment and tea; and the Great Missenden Cottagers' and Labourers' Friendly Society. In August there was the School Annual Treat, followed by the Methodist Sunday School Treat. In November there was the Primitive Methodist Sunday School Anniversary.'

Ann N. Marchant, *Ballinger*

I clearly remember holidays with my family at a small farm in Ballinger during the first decade of the century.

Besides the farm, Mr Bachelor owned a brick kiln and our chief joy was sliding down the shute used for the bricks.

In those days we could safely bowl our hoops along the country lanes, and as a great treat Mr Bachelor would let one or other of us accompany him on his occasional errands in the pony trap to the little towns of Chesham or Tring.

10

Sanitation was primitive—an outside privy with cut-up newspaper as ammunition hanging on the door. My mother, feeling this was a bit rough on our tender rear ends, enquired of Mr Lewington who owned the village general store if he had a toilet roll. He regretted but politely asked if he could oblige with a newspaper . . .!

One dull Sunday afternoon, we children were playing a game of Halma in our sitting room, when a sudden commotion in the yard sent us out to see what it was all about. A large sow had got loose. The crisis over, we went back to our game only to find that it had been carefully put away and a Bible placed on top—a gentle rebuke from Mrs Bachelor who was a strict Baptist and obviously didn't hold with our heathen ways!

M. Webber, *Little Chalfont*

Bledlow Station was opened at the beginning of 1864. The first Station Master was Mr John Greenaway; his son kept the Seven Stars public house opposite and had seven children. The pub was quite small, so every night beds were set up in the station waiting room for some of the children and removed before the first passenger train arrived in the morning.

In those days at Bledlow there were thirty-two trains a day, the station being manned by the master and two porters. Goods sent from the station were varied and in large quantities, ranging from two tons of Aylesbury ducks a week during the season to trawler blocks from James Walker's timber mills at Longwick which amounted to some two hundred tons a week, and milk from farmers in Bledlow and Henton. Many trucks of wood were unloaded at

Bledlow and paper in large quantities sent in and out from the paper mills. In those days, rags were chopped at nearby North Mill in preparation for paper making at the Paper Mills. Then on a very sad day in January 1963, the station was closed after a busy and useful life of ninety-nine years. The line is still used to supply Thame Petrol Depot, B.P. and Shell.

J. Walker, *Bledlow*

Mother Shipton the prophetess said:
'They who live and do abide
Will see Bledlow church fall into the Lyde.
Those that live and do remain
Shall see Bledlow church build up again.'

Annie Hobbs, *Bledlow*

Bledlow Ridge

At Bledlow Ridge forty years ago the dwellings were few and far between, often tucked away down a side lane, and the population was little more than four hundred. Cattle and sheep grazed serenely and safely on neat grass verges.

It was a marvellously tidy place, conservation being practised more than it was preached in those days. Although there was no organised refuse collection, no unsightly rubbish littered the countryside and leaving paper litter was a punishable offence for the reason that it might blow about and frighten horses and bring some poor creature to an untimely end. All waste material usually found its way back to the land. No milk bottle problem existed either for, armed with a milk jug, one went to the nearest farm and queued at the dairy door after the morning or evening milking.

12

Water was a valuable commodity. Time was when on these hills rain water was the only source of supply and was stored in large underground tanks usually mis-called 'wells'. For watering of cattle most farmers relied on ponds. The hard water which now gushes through Bledlow Ridge taps certainly has its recommendations. The quality of tank water varied to a great extent; it was assumed that the rain itself was pure, but its collection and after-care were a different matter. A time of drought was deemed the best for descending to the bottom of a tank to remove any remaining water, and an amazing assortment of debris would have collected there. The concrete lining was thoroughly wiped, all down-pipes, catch pits and guttering cleaned out and examined. Then one waited for the rain. Thunder rains were usually impregnated with dirt which had to settle before use. Rain off a galvanised tin roof was cleanest and quickly collected. Second best was rain from slates or tiles but that collected from thatching was usually discoloured and difficult to catch efficiently. For this reason families in thatched cottages drank surface water for preference. There was no drainage. Only a few cottages had sinks in the kitchen. Most cottages had sizeable gardens and usually every bit was put to practical use. Often pigs were kept, either to sell or for the household. Pig-keeping helped to keep up the cycle of conservation in the garden. No chemical other than lime was applied to the soil.

Monday morning early found the few industries of the village already working. The blacksmith at The Old Forge was clanging at his anvil, the chair bodger was at his pole lathe, the farm labourer leading his team of horses, the chimney sweep with tackle in his pony-drawn cart, schoolchildren, packets of lunch sandwiches in hand, walking the lanes to school. At his last was the shoe-maker, locally called a 'snob'.

With the population of Bledlow Ridge at now more than one thousand many of the picturesque thatched

13

and flint cottages have disappeared, modern homes having taken their place, and much of the pasture has been built upon. Gone too is the old windmill, but happily the Mill House, three hundred years old, still remains a sturdy structure, reminder of a former way of life. Gone too is a vast wild cherry tree of tremendous girth that stood at the corner of a lane dwarfing a cottage beneath it.

D. Rogers, *Bledlow Ridge*

Great Missenden

My grandfather lived at Sedges Farm and my family lived near by. We enjoyed the company of three young cousins. This number was greatly increased during the school holidays when several 'town' cousins came to stay on the farm, and local children joined in too.

Extra men were employed at harvest-time, and work went on for several days. When the threshing machine was working in the rick-yard all the children were armed with sticks, with the intention of slaying the mice as they were disturbed. We were always rewarded with delicious farmhouse cake and lemonade and the harvesters had homemade wine—not old enough to be potent, although there were times at the end of the day when their feet used to 'wander' a little.

Not only did we enjoy glorious long summers in those days but we also had extremely hard winters. One year we had prolonged snow and frost, and heavy snowdrifts completely covered parts of a nearby lane including the hedges, and a very large carthorse walked from his meadow across the snow into another farmer's meadow.

I suppose Great Missenden has altered least of all the villages in this district. It was not so very many years ago that the local baker baked his bread in an enormous oven heated by solid fuels, and how delicious it was too. It was delivered to customers by pony and trap several times a week. Often at tea-time the muffin-man would call, ringing his bell as he approached the house.

On occasions, I was taken by my grandfather to Missenden Abbey to walk round the beautiful gardens. It has a long and interesting history, as had Sedges Farm where I spent so many happy days during school holidays.

In fact there were rather strange inscriptions on the walls of the three attic rooms in the roof of the farm, believed to be inscribed by monks. Unfortunately the old stairway to the attics has been replaced and some of the wall removed and likewise the attics have been altered and the inscriptions covered or removed by the builders. The farmhouse still stands, commanding a lovely view across the hills, with Great Missenden church nestling in the hillside.

I also remember the many gipsy families who camped in the shelter of the thick high hedges in what is still called Gipsy Lane near the farm. The same families came and went year after year, the men sometimes stone-picking in the fields before the ploughing and sowing.

Ivy Smith, *Great Kingshill (Evening)*

Before the coming of the railway in 1892, Great Missenden was quite a small rural community and the centre of a considerable agricultural district. Nevertheless, it boasted no less than twelve public houses in its one main street. This sometimes led to quite riotous behaviour round the village green in Church Street, on Saturdays and holidays. A travelling fair often occupied the green also, to add to the excitement.

The old High Street was cobbled and used by a considerable amount of horse traffic. This caused it to be encrusted by a deep layer of manure. In dry weather the shop windows had to be barricaded against the flying filth. The Oxford to London coach came through the village daily, with its four horses and a postillion blowing his horn.

The fire engine was kept behind one of the inns and was drawn by horses lent by the riding stables.

There was a Town Crier, called Tomlin, with his handbell who called the local news and dates of auctions, agricultural shows and the time and the weather.

A lamplighter went through the village each evening lighting the lamps for a few hours of darkness.

A muffin-man walked from Chesham with a tray of muffins, covered with a white cloth, balanced on his head.

A horse-brake used to meet the London train on Sundays and take passengers on a circular drive in the country, passing Chequers and on to Wendover where tea was provided at the Shoulder of Mutton, then back to Great Missenden and the train for an inclusive fare of half-a-crown.

The butcher, who was also the slaughterer, made large quantities of lard and dripping and customers brought their own bowls to be filled. The great treat on Wednesdays used to be hot dripping toast.

A well-known figure of those times was a drover called Jesse, who drove cattle from the market at Aylesbury to the slaughter-house. Jesse sustained himself by calling at the various hostelries on his route. When he arrived at the Black Horse on the outskirts of the village, he would leave the cattle outside while he enjoyed his final drink. It was a favourite trick of a number of children living nearby, to chase the cattle into the handy village pond and watch with delight a somewhat bemused Jesse looking for his herd.

The bakery, recently closed, belonged to the Clark family for over two hundred years. They also owned the mill, which was known as Deep Mill, and ground the wheat for the flour. Housewives used to bring their Christmas turkeys and cakes, and large joints and pies to the bakehouse to be cooked in the bread oven.

The Squire's four sisters, the Misses Carrington, who lived at Missenden Abbey, were very kind but autocratic ladies. When they visited in the village, the women were expected to appear at their doors in clean aprons, and curtsey. On one occasion when two women in the street failed to do this they were asked 'whether their knees were stiff'. Children were invited each spring to a Snowdrop Tea at the Squire's mansion, now a College of Adult Education. They were allowed to pick as many snowdrops as they liked in the Park and were then entertained to tea in the house.

Lacemakers sat three or four together in the bay windows of houses in Church Street. They used 'chaddy pots', similar to a warming pan, filled with hot coals and tucked under their skirts for warmth. When it was dark the group sat round one candle which had a special glass reflector. A salesman collected the completed lace periodically for very small sums.

Straw plaiting was also done by the cottagers at home, for the Luton hat trade. They used to sit in their doorways plaiting the wet straw, which resulted in very sore hands.

The Buckingham Arms (now the National Westminster Bank) had some very interesting people always staying there. There is in existence still a

17

visitors' book dating back to the early 1900's which is filled with comment and drawings and some poems. One party of people who stayed there regularly were some strolling players who performed plays and melodramas in an old building in the yard behind the Red Lion. One villager worked after school hours at this hotel as 'Boots' and stable boy from the age of eight.

The village school headmaster of those days insisted that as the district was an agricultural one all boys must be taught to cultivate a pole of land. They were allowed to sell their produce, which sometimes came to as much as 12s 6d which they collected at Christmas.

Members of *Great Missenden*

Hyde Heath

When I was young, the highlight of our school year was not so much the last day of the summer term as a day when we held our May Revels. The First of May was always too cold and wet, for the celebrations were held on the common adjoining the school. The performers all had parents and grandparents, aunts and uncles, who made up the village community.

Preparations for May Day Revels began about the middle of the Easter term, as they included learning extracts from works of Mendelssohn and Shakespeare, all of which were rehearsed day after day until perfect. The lucky girl to be crowned Queen of the May was elected by popular vote from all her school friends, and other 'star' parts like Jack-in-the-Green, Chief Courtier and Queen's attendants were allocated.

The evening before, we gathered the greenery and wild flowers with which to 'dress' our wooden hoops, make garlands and the Royal Crown. White dresses

18

were ready for the girls to wear with coloured sun bonnets, and white shirts and grey shorts for the boys, except for 'Jack', who had a special green outfit. On May morning my sisters and I carried our dressed hoops and other flowers, except for the years when, in turn, we had been chosen to be Queen.

At the school everyone was busy setting up the throne on the common, and the piano was somehow pushed outside the school playground. If the wind happened to be a bit strong it was always just too far away to be heard well.

It was lovely dancing on the green grass after so many rehearsals on the hard playground. After the Queen's procession and the crowning ceremony the real revels began. Many were the country dances in which the flowered hoops were held aloft and swayed from side to side, and there was also the Maypole dancing. Such intricate patterns we weaved with those pretty ribbons, and woe betide anyone who made a mistake so that the ribbons had to be dropped and the dance abandoned! In between dances songs were sung, about the cuckoo, spring and the beauty of the flowers. The Revels ended with a speech by the Queen, telling her subjects to go home and look forward to the next merry meeting.

Enid Picton, *Hyde Heath*

Fifty years ago, the common at Hyde Heath was one mass of gorse. There were no trees, but the footpaths that led in different directions were kept clear by the cottagers for walking. Hyde Heath was only a small hamlet but it had three public houses, the Red Cow, the Eagle and the Plough, which at that time only sold beer and porter. Eventually two were made redundant and the remaining one, the Plough, is now

Straw plaits

fully licensed. Troy Cottage was at that time the bakery where the inhabitants went to collect their bread. Flint Cottage was the only general stores and post office.

Fruit was picked and taken to London by horse and cart and sold in Nottinghill Gate market. Most of the men in the village worked on the farms, some of the women did straw plaiting which was delivered to Luton by horse and trap to be made into hats. I can also remember an old resident, when water was short and having only soft water from the tanks, going to Little Missenden with his horse and cart, taking a barrel to get the spring water for drinking and selling it at one penny a bucket. Several women used to go stone picking, also thistle punching for one shilling a day. There was also a small chair factory, behind the Red Cow. There were less than a hundred houses in the village at that time, lit only by paraffin lamps and candles, and having no baths.

Ellen Morton (died February, 1975), *Hyde Heath*

Lacey Green

Mrs Adams was born in Lacey Green eighty-five years ago and still lives in the house the family moved to when she was three years old. Her father was a travelling chair-man, journeying far to obtain orders for chairs, but he died when his daughter was not much over eight years of age. In order not to accept the Parish Charity and be known as a pauper, she and her mother made lace or did beadwork so as to pay their way. Lace makers earned ½d or ¾d per hour and supplied the cottons, but beadwork paid more, and Mrs Adams can remember sitting up all night with three others round a table, all working on one dress which was required for a particular time for

20

the theatre. A very small needle was used for bead work, made of steel but called a 'straw needle'. When young she used to suffer from toothache and found that if she stuck a needle into the tooth it used to ease the pain. Eventually she went to the dentist and had the tooth removed and the dentist showed her the tooth with half a beading needle still in it.

F.H. Adams, *Loosley Row & Lacey Green*

An old lady who used to live in another Bucks village recalled teasing an elderly lady there about the young good-looking man who frequently called, to be told 'That's my son, he was the last rubbings of the dough'!

M. Griffith, *Loosley Row & Lacey Green*

Little Kingshill

Walking was the usual way of getting around, although on Saturdays a pony and trap ran through the village. This eventually led to a horse and brake which could carry seven people at a time. For private use one could hire a horse and brougham from the Nag's Head Inn. The noise of the horns and bugles could be heard in Little Kingshill when the stage coach passed through Great Missenden. The horses were changed at the White Lion.

Little Kingshill was a small village but in many ways self-sufficient with two shops (one was also the bakery, and the old bread ovens were pulled down in 1973 to make way for more new houses), two public houses, a home laundry, a village hall, the old day school and also a private day and boarding school called St Christopher's. In a house near the common a bodger used to turn chair legs for the famous Windsor chairs made in High Wycombe and sent to London by horse and cart.

Those who were children early this century mostly remember the highlights of a year as May Day with the Maypole, Empire Day and other festivals. Sundays were also very important when everyone attended Church or Chapel in their best clothes, often twice a day. The Baptist Church in the village was always full upstairs and downstairs. Prizes were given for regular attendance. Little Kingshill formed a Women's Institute just after the first World War and the Cricket Club was also formed over sixty years ago.

Great Missenden was, we thought, a gay place. At the rear of the George Hotel was a cage in which the drunken men were kept overnight before they faced court in the morning.

The District Nurse lived in Great Missenden and she rode a bicycle before owning a car. As she had to be fetched by walking or cycling it could be quite a time before she reached the patient in any emergency. Cycling became a popular pastime and one notable always rode a penny-farthing.

There have never been any street lights in Little Kingshill but one member's father was the lamplighter in High Wycombe and lit every gas lamp with the long pole every night.

Members of *Little Kingshill*

Little Missenden   At the turn of the century in Little Missenden, William Folliott cared for the pastoral needs of his flock. This well loved cleric of Irish descent was a familiar figure as he walked his Parish, a never-ending supply of peppermints in his pocket to be shared with children and grown-ups alike. He also dispensed his church's charities to his poor parishioners—lengths of flannel to make warm petticoats, and coal for the needy. Six loaves of bread were distributed by the clerk to deserving parishioners attending morning service. These loaves, decorating the font top, existed until a few years ago, the number getting gradually less as the price of bread increased until this present day when the Bird's Charity money only provides one harvest loaf.

When King Edward VII came to stay at Earl Howe's home at Penn, the children were given a holiday from school and walked to Penn to see King Edward. The Reverend Folliott died at the vicarage opposite the Church, and with many a quaking knee the school children filed past his coffin to pay their last respects.

The village school, now one of the smallest in Buckinghamshire, took in large numbers of children from the villages around. The schoolmistress of those days was a real martinet. A favourite punishment was to make a dullard stand in front of his fellow pupils holding as many as twelve slates on his head. What was considered even more cruel was the administering of 'the cat of nine tails' to a young boy at this time. He had stolen farthings from one of the village shops to buy some food. His mother had spent the family housekeeping on that 'Demon Drink'!

The village up to the First World War boasted four shops, four farms, two inns, a bakery, a mill, a smithy and a post office. At Smithy Cottage one of the two old fire insurance plaques can be seen. This was the only cottage that would have the services of the fire engine of that time, before the days of the National Fire Service.

The village green was first laid with turves brought

from Mr Pembroke Stephens' former home near Durham. A lamp was installed to light the green, but a village row broke out as to who should pay for the paraffin, and so the lamp went unlit and during the hours of darkness wheels, hooves and feet encroached on the green and spoilt its former beauty.

The Misbourne was a fast flowing stream in those days, turning the mill wheel. The Sibleys kept the mill here and as well as others along the Misbourne, and their Christian charity is still spoken of. The remains of their breakfasts were always taken over to the occupants of the Mill End Cottages.

Life was hard for most of the villagers of those days. Many village women tried to help out a meagre existence by straw plaiting, roller blind making or stone picking and breaking. This latter employment brought them 6d per yard.

The Berkeley Coach travelling between Wendover—the Missendens—the Chalfonts and Uxbridge could be boarded, but the fare was between five and six shillings. The first motor car to break the rural peace of the village was driven by the much loved medico, Dr Gardener, who, resplendent in top hat and morning coat and with his buttonhole of Parma violets, always dispensed his physics and good advice in equal portions to his admiring patients.

Dr Bates resided at the Manor. He is remembered as belonging to the notorious 'Hell Fire Club' of West Wycombe. The Manor is a beautiful part-Tudor building with spacious grounds through which the Misbourne flows. One of the owners produced so many daughters that the two front pews were needed to house them for Sunday services. Latterly Lady Alice Ashley and Brigadier Roger Peake, both with histories of service to our Royal Family, have given a lead to village life.

The church's most famous possession is the St Christopher Mural, which came to light during the 1930's, when the Reverend William Henry Davis, scratching away with a penknife at the plastered walls, uncovered some of the most perfect examples of medieval wall paintings not only of St Christopher but St Catherine and the Wheel and a Crucifixion scene as well.

Joan Smith, *Little Missenden*

I was born in Loosley Row, one of twelve children brought up in a small cottage where cooking was done over the fire and in a brick oven which was let into the wall. The fire was lit inside the oven and fed with long 'kindlings' and when it was hot enough the burning embers were raked out into a bucket, the food to be cooked placed on a spade and let down onto the hot bricks—things like Backbone Pie, Crittens Puddings, jugged pigs' lights, and bread of course. The bread and puddings were made from the flour obtained from the gleaning after harvesting was finished, taken first to Lacey Green Mill for the first grinding and then to Princes Risborough for milling into flour.

Beatrice Dormer, *Loosley Row & Lacey Green*

The Misses Gomme lived in Loosley Row down by the foundry where there was a public well. Most houses relied on water collected from the roof for ordinary use but drinking water was fetched from the well; in a dry spell people came from as far as a mile away over steep footpaths with a yoke and two buckets. As children, the Misses Gomme went to

25

Lodge Hill on Good Fridays with fizzy lemonade and hot cross-buns. There was a dell there, and it was said that if you could run five times round the dell, holding your breath, you would meet the devil! No-one ever managed it, to their knowledge!

Miss Hilda Gomme was a postwoman, without uniform or boots supplied, delivering and collecting post on foot. She carried a whistle which she had to blow when emptying the box so that people who had forgotten to post their letters could run out with them; the time she could wait was specified. She suffered a good deal with chilblains and there was always the danger of dogs—one Alsatian jumped over a gate and bit her in the shoulder right through all her clothes; there was no compensation, it was all part of the job. Miss Hilda delivered post for fifty-four years and retired at the age of seventy-nine when it was estimated she had walked something like 84,000 miles in her job.

Miss Madge Gomme worked as a 'between maid' at Loosley House, living in and subject to the discipline of the cook who was strict and did not like the girls going out in an evening, although they would get out if they could.

Hilda and Madge Gomme (written by Madeline Cleaver),
Loosley Row & Lacey Green.

*Princes
Risborough*

Princes Risborough was a small market town of four or five streets when I first came to visit my great aunt in the year 1895. My aunt's farmhouse was in the High Street, with the barns and fields behind, and is now a jeweller's shop and coal office downstairs with a dentist in the rooms above. The old barns are now used by an engineering firm. There was another

Whiteleaf Cross

farmhouse up on the opposite side of the street with their fields and buildings beyond, and still another farm called Town Farm round the corner off the Market Place.

There were many public houses in the High Street, most of them licensed for market day only. At the top of this street was the blacksmith's forge, and where Lloyds Bank is now was a very nice inn. There were more inns and taverns in Duke Street, Church Street and Bell Street as this seemed to be the only means of recreation and sociability enjoyed by the men.

There were two schools in the town, one was the National and the other was run by the Church, and in those early days parents had to pay for books. If they could not afford to pay, children did not go. The man who worked on my great aunt's farm could neither read nor write but was skilled in farm work. His wife was a beautiful lace maker. Mothers taught their daughters this craft.

The first of May brought a special gaiety to the town. Children would rise early and dance round the streets carrying poles festooned with garlands they had made the evening before. Lots of cowslips were gathered for this. Two children would carry a pole and they would all sing 'Here we come a-Maying'.

27

They would gather up the coppers, thrown to them from doors and windows, with great glee, and would no doubt spend them later at the Spring Fair.

There was at that time a Charity which gave a black dress to several deserving poor and bereaved women once a year. They were fitted, the dresses were made at the dressmakers, and then at a special church service the dresses were presented to them.

I remember going to the woods to watch the bodgers at work. They were self-employed men who bought the rights of certain areas, then set up their benches and tools next to the trees. Their skilled eye would select the right branch and bend and turn it into chair parts on the spot. These were sent to the chair factory at High Wycombe.

Mabel Gertrude Rodgers (aged 92), *Princes Risborough*

Wendover   My earliest memory is of the bonfire on Coombe Hill to celebrate the end of the Boer War and the return of two local men from South Africa. They were met at the railway station by the whole village headed by the village brass band, together with the horse-drawn fire engine on which they were conveyed to their homes.

Ploughing matches were a frequent occurrence. The horses of the entering teams had manes and tails plaited with ribbons or straw, brasses highly polished, and sometimes they wore little straw hats—possibly for protection against flies.

Boys on the farms were also used for crow scaring. They sat on a fence and shouted:

'I'll knock up with my clappers
I'll knock you down back'ards,
Shoo all away.'

28

The clappers were similar to the present football fans' rattle.

Instead of the traditional Maypole, children tied bunches of flowers to a stick and sang at the doors, 'Maypole Day—please give me a ha'penny and then I'll run away'. The money they collected was spent at the May Fair on 13 May.

Parish Council elections aroused strong interest and local wags produced a pamphlet portraying the entrants as horses with prospective form and possible results.

Parliamentary elections were even more lively. Most people's political convictions were well known and opposing parties toured the village at night with colour wash and posters. We found our windows coloured yellow and blue, the Rothschild colours, and over the door a huge Liberal poster. If the gangs met, the paste and colour wash was used on each other.

Vagrants walking from Aylesbury workhouse to Amersham would call at a house for hot water for tea cans and then ask for a spoonful of tea to put in it, and beg a slice of bread elsewhere.

Other casual visitors were organ grinders with their barrel organs with a monkey on top, German bands (but these disappeared in 1914), a scissors grinder with portable grindstone, an Italian with a melodeon, a lamplighter, and a carrier who chased the children with a knife. We also had a Town Crier.

Children's games were played chiefly in the roads. The boys had iron hoops guided with iron hooks called skimmers; marbles—called Doddies; pop-guns—hollowed elder stems with rose hips for ammunition; tops—spun by winding string round and then whipped along, often causing broken windows. The girls had wooden hoops; five stones—called Dabbers; cats' cradle; and singing games—Nuts in May, Oranges and Lemons and Green Gravel. This latter game was a circle with one child in the centre. They sang:

'Green gravel, green gravel, the grass is so green,
The fairest young lady that ever was seen.
Come back, love, come back, love, your true
    love is dead.
I send you a letter and choose you instead.'

The centre child chose a partner and the circle revolved singing:
'Now you are married we wish you joy'.

E. Eldridge, W. Hibberd, *Wendover*

III
Buckingham
Hundred

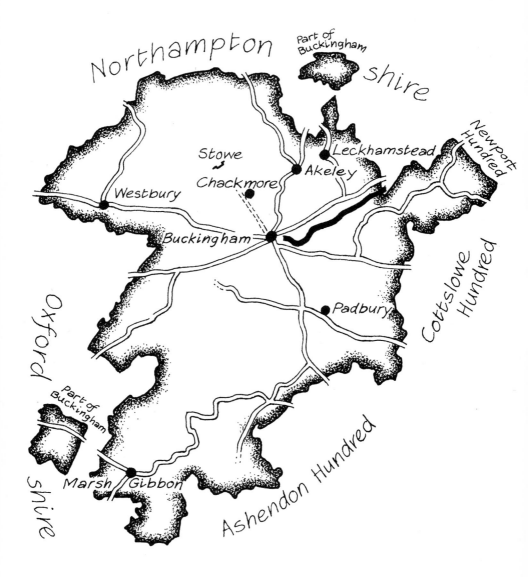

Northampton shire

Part of Buckingham

Newport Hundred

Stowe

Leckhamstead

Chackmore

Akeley

Westbury

Buckingham

Cottslowe Hundred

Padbury

Oxford shire

Part of Buckingham

Marsh Gibbon

Ashendon Hundred

At the turn of the century, this little village in north Bucks was almost entirely self-supporting. There were two general stores, a butcher, a baker, who was also landlord of the Greyhound, a builder and undertaker, a coal and wood merchant, two cobblers, a tailor and a wheelwright who carried on his trade in the yard of the Bull and Butcher.

There was a headmaster and two assistants in the little school, built in 1854, and a new church built on the site of an early thirteenth century one.

In addition, there was a thriving pottery where simple bowls, puncheons and flowerpots were made from clay obtained nearby, and hand-made bricks in sufficient quantities to build cottages in the village. Every Saturday a load of flowerpots, bowls and other crocks were taken to Buckingham market and from time to time into the surrounding villages.

Bread was made at the Greyhound by John Miller. When the bread was taken out of the ovens, villagers took their pies, cakes and stews to be cooked in the residual heat. On Sunday mornings the ovens were heated specially so that Sunday dinners could be cooked there, for the price of a penny-halfpenny.

Milk was fetched from the Church Farm where the farmer's wife, Mrs Winterburn, on Christmas Day stood a large basket of oranges by her door and gave one to each child who came for their milk.

In August, the village feast was held. The local showman, Sheppard by name, who lived at Blisworth when not 'on the road', brought all his gear and set it up in a field allowed for the purpose. Swings, roundabouts, shooting-gallery, hoop-la, were all manned by members of his family.

Akeley has always been a village of sturdy independence, with small farms and cottage industries. The nearest it came to having a squire was in 1873, when a gentleman named Pilgrim bought some land and built an Elizabethan-style residence in Akeley Wood. He also became patron of the living. His widow, Mrs Pilgrim, is still a legend in the memories of the older parishioners, for she was a strange woman of strong evangelistic tendencies, with generous impulses towards the village while seeking, by missioners and others, to instil the rigid code of her own beliefs.

The school children were taken in two wagons every Christmas by one of the farmers for a sumptuous tea and Christmas tree in the 'riding-school', now used as a gymnasium, since the house was converted to a preparatory school about forty years ago. At this Christmas treat each boy was given a muffler and the girls a doll. These dolls were beautifully dressed by Mrs Pilgrim's lady's maid. On May Day the children assembled there with their garlands to be judged by Mrs Pilgrim, and a doll given as a prize.

When Mrs Pilgrim died, she was buried at her expressed wish with feet towards the west instead of the east; her reason being that when she rose again at the Last Day, she would be facing towards her old home. On the stone slab, encircled by iron posts and chain around her grave, are two words only; Anna Pilgrim.

Lady Verney of Claydon House took an interest in the village school and provided wall-pictures which she changed periodically. They were usually by Landseer and contemporary artists.

The traditional country craft, Bucks lace, was encouraged by a 'lace school' in a thatched cottage which was then opposite the Greyhound but which was pulled down later to make room for Council houses. Many of the village girls were taught there.

Akeley has a record of longevity, many living to their late nineties but none as yet exceeding that of Ann Clarke, who died in 1773 at the age of 104 as her tombstone shows. The story goes that one old lady who lost a daughter aged seventy lamented, 'Ah! I never did think I should rear her', and a retired postmistress remembers a mother and son, he aged seventy, both drawing the old age pension in the 1950's.

The old people remember the characters that village life produced and fostered, such as Jonas Knibbs, one-time sexton and verger, who was employed as milkman at Manor Farm and spent his Sundays in a frenzy of changing his clothes as he fulfilled the day's obligations: from milking to church, back to milking and then church again. Indeed, clothes were such a part of Sunday observance that children of careful parents might change from 'everyday' to 'Sunday best' three and four times.

Becky Knibbs—this surname was noted in the church registers for over two hundred years—lived in Duck End. She was a tall old woman who constantly wore a sun-bonnet and made medicaments from herbs kept fiercely secret.

Where the children once found excitement in watching the Duke of Grafton drive four-in-hand through the village, mothers now watch them anxiously cross the road where the great lorries and giant containers lumber along.

Plans for a new school are in preparation, modern houses stare brashly across the fields, the many little duck ponds have long been filled in, but to many of its older inhabitants Akeley is still the best place to live.

Edith Victoria Cox, *Akeley (Evening)*

Chackmore

Chackmore is a little village off Stowe Avenue. In its centre is an elm tree, of which this saying has been handed down for generations:— 'if no baby is born in the village during a year the tree will fall down'. It still stands!

In my childhood the village had a carrier who set out on a Saturday morning with his four-wheeled cart, pulled by a fine chestnut horse, for Dadford, three miles away. He collected shopping orders and sometimes passengers from both villages, journeyed back to Chackmore and on to Buckingham to pick up the shopping which he delivered from house to house in the afternoon.

At Whitsun we looked forward to the gipsies invading a farmer's field with roundabouts and all the fun of the fair.

The annual Harvest Supper was a great event. My mother cooked a huge ham in her copper, and salt beef in the big boiler on the old black grate. Barrels of beer were rolled up to the farmyard from the Queen's Head inn. Then dancing followed in the gaily decorated barn.

On Boxing Day we always greeted the arrival of 'the Mummers' with the dancing bear and money-box.

On a Saturday morning children walked the three miles to a Stowe farm to purchase half a gallon of skim milk for twopence to make the Sunday milk puddings.

Dadford is the village of the parish of Stowe. In the old days it consisted of about three families, all intermarried. The schoolmistress's daughter kept the little post office and sold cigarettes.

F.M. Fricker, *Dadford*

In the first decade of this century I left my home in London to pay a visit to some relatives in north Bucks in the village of Leckhampstead. This visit was never terminated and from the age of four I spent the next fifty years in the same cottage that became my home.

In the fifty years up to the 1914-18 war, our village life had changed very little, except when the Education Act provided free schooling. Till then our village school, built about 1850, had received such scholars whose parents could afford the few coppers a week required. The children walked the mile or so to school, where they were taught the three R's, and a smattering of history and geography by question and answer. By the time I arrived, the school was properly equipped by one qualified teacher and an assistant. Between forty and fifty children attended. The village green was our playground.

My great-uncle, Walter Hurst, was the eldest of five children born at Wood House, my great-grandfather being a woodman, as were generations of Hursts before him. My uncle tenanted a small holding of twenty-six acres and our house overlooked the green with the brook running by. He also carried on the wood business held by his forefathers, in which he employed one or two men, cutting down the undergrowth, keeping the ridings clear and utilising the wood for faggots, bean poles, pea-sticks, hurdles and rakes, which he sold in the surrounding villages. He took loads of oak-bark to the tanners in Northampton for use in the leather industry. Only horses were used for transport, and the load would start off early in the morning with probably a stop at Towcester and Blisworth to rest horses and men on the way.

We also had two 'carriage' horses as my uncle supplied carriages for the rectory nearby and was also the local 'carrier' to Buckingham on market days.

In addition my aunt kept the post office, so we

were always involved in the life of the village, my uncle being also a churchwarden, school manager and parish councillor.

The rectory and its occupants were the centre of the village. Our rector was a son of the Bishop of Winchester, his wife the eldest daughter of a Scottish peer. Their house—the largest in the village—had its complement of servants, with a gardener and handy boy. The servant girls employed were usually from other villages. Our own girls were 'put out' to places chosen by the rector's wife, or they found their own from a little registry office in Buckingham. Some men worked at the iron foundry at Deanshanger, a few cycled to the Wolverton Railway Carriage Works but most were employed on the land in some capacity.

Busby, the greengrocer, came round with his horse and trolley from Buckingham to all the surrounding villages, and the children and mothers gathered with their cans and baskets of fruit, glad of the twopence a lb he gave them.

In January, the choir and bellringers had their supper, an enormous round of boiled salt beef and a huge roasted leg of pork; beetroots were cooked, peeled and sliced, Christmas puddings made and boiled, and on the day, there was a marathon potato-peeling.

Lent was a special time. We had week-night services when the local parsons 'exchanged pulpits', and usually a visiting missionary would give us a lantern lecture in the newly built parish room.

Spring sent us round the hedges 'vi-letting'. We went in groups, the elders hastening ahead to bag the best patches. They knew from experience where the rarer white and 'grey' (mauve) ones grew, even the more secret and treasured spots where deep pink ones were to be found.

By Good Friday, the primroses were out in Leckhampstead Wood and a number of the girls would make a special journey to gather them for decorating the church for Easter Day.

38

Early on Easter morning, the bellringers mustered to ring a peal. The Church, filled with spring flowers, looked strangely new and beautiful. Self-conscious youths and maidens were there to make their first communion as confirmations always took place in Lent.

Figs were an inescapable part of Palm Sunday, and the hot cross-buns brought round by the bakers on Good Friday morning. We had Easter Eggs too, but they were mostly the cardboard type, filled with some little novelty and tied with ribbon.

The next red-letter day after Easter was May Day. Garden flowers were begged from those who were willing to give, and we searched the banks and hedgerows for blue bells, cowslip and marsh marigolds—we called them 'water bubbles'. The simplest May garland was a bunch of flowers tied to the end of a long stick, with streamers of ribbon. Boys had these. Girls preferred two wooden hoops crossed between each other, or a child's small chair, with willow wands fastened over the back and arms in arches. This foundation was covered first in moss, then with tiny bunches of flowers. It was usual to make a cowslip ball to hang from the top of the middle arch and, to soar above it, such may as could be found together with blooms of Crown Imperial or 'Crown of Pearls'. The grandest doll that could be round was fastened securely in the whole garland veiled in a curtain to hide it from curious eyes while in transit. Two of the biggest girls carried the garland, the one selected to be Queen had a sash tied across from shoulder to waist after the style of the 'Garter' ribbon and she carried the money box. This was the song we sang:

'Good morning, young ladies and gentlemen,
I wish you a happy May.
I have come to show you my May garland
Because it is May Day.

'A branch of may I have brought you
And at your door it stands.
It is but a sprout, but is well
   spread about
By the work of our Lord's hands.

'Now take the Bible in your hands,
And read the chapter through,
And when the day of judgement comes
God will remember you.

'And now I've finished my little
   short song
I can no longer stay.
So God bless you all, both great
   and small
In the merry month of May.'

It was a tradition that the girls wore white on Whit Sunday.

Children looked forward to hay-time, helping with the preparations for it, particularly in carrying tea. Leckhampstead is a large village in acreage though relatively small in population. Tea might have to be carried to Wicken Wood or up to Lillingstone Lovell. There was not so much arable land just before the first world war. Many farmers had put down to grass much that had been ploughed land, as they did again between the wars. There were no subsidies then.

During the day, the horse-drawn machine had cut the swathes, and by late afternoon, and the next day, the men and women workers walked in rows with their rakes, turning the swathes. The women wore long skirts and aprons and perhaps a sun-bonnet or a man's cap on their heads. After tea in the hayfield some of the men left to do the milking, then the bigger children took over. Later, when the hay was fit to carry, there were long rides in the empty waggons.

Harvesting at the turn
of the century

Towards the end of September, Harvest Festival
was held. There were always masses of fruit, flowers
and vegetables and of course the traditional sheaf of
corn to stand in the chancel. One could always be
sure of a well-packed church for Harvest Festival. The
bellringers always stayed to this service—although
they were inclined on ordinary occasions to shuffle
out of the belfry-door as soon as they had 'rung down'.

The villagers by the late autumn had gathered in
every hedgerow harvest; blackberries, sloes for wine-
making, mushrooms culled from the dew-drenched
fields, walnuts staining the fingers, and 'conkers'.

My aunt started making her puddings by the last
week of Trinity. A night or two before Christmas we
heard the handbell ringers outside the door. After
playing a few tunes they were invited in and given
beer or wine and cake. Then they rang again before
they left.

Maids Moreton ringers called too: they were more
proficient than our Leckhampstead ringers who were
somewhat jerky in their performance.

We always sat up to hear the church bells ring the
old year out and the new year in. This was echoed
from the distance by Wicken or Maids Moreton
belfries. Sometimes we could hear Buckingham bells
too. We didn't practise any superstitious rituals.

Edith Victoria Cox, *Lillingstones & Akeley*

41

Weather Lore

If grass do grow in Janu'air
'Twill grow the worse the rest of the year

Half the straw and half the hay
Must be in the barn on Candlemas Day (Feb 2)

Fogs in March—frost in May

There are always twenty one fine days in October

Ice in November, enough to bear a duck,
The rest of the winter all mud and muck.

Anne Robertson, *Marsh Gibbon*

At the turn of the century Marsh Gibbon was noted for its large proportion of thatched cottages and barns, and most of the farm workers of the village could thatch.

House thatching was a business of its own as carried on by the Carter family and this was their only means of earning a living. The straw was supplied by local farmers, as was the willow used for making sprays and pegs. This craft was very skilled and the Carters travelled on foot to neighbouring villages and borrowed ladders from the farmers for their own use.

The process involved was that the straw of the best wheat was shaken out into a heap and wetted, yealmed into bundles to take up the ladder, laid on the roof (working from the bottom upwards) until they had completed a 'stolch' or strip, then it was pegged on, working from right to left across one side of the roof. If a good straw was used and the work

42

well done a thatched roof has been known to last thirty years, but the normal length would be twenty years. The main part of the houses nowadays are covered with wire netting to protect the thatch from birds. Mr Owen Carter, now retired and living in the village, gave me details of prices his father charged. They were rather staggering, 4s 6d to 5s 6d per hundred square feet of roof.

As a farmer's daughter, I recall trips to the corn fields in the summer when the corn was being cut with the binder into sheaves, then shocked into stooks to dry out before being carried on horse-drawn wagons and made into a rick in readiness for threshing in the winter months. Some of my father's straw has been used to thatch houses in this village.

Eileen Chambers, *Marsh Gibbon*

My father-in-law, now ninety-two, has a few tales to tell. In the school holidays he was given 1d per week and sent to a little cottage school which only held about ten children. The wives in those days were busy with the lace pillows to earn a few extra pence and they often started the day with a hymn they chose at the school. Because it was a favourite 'Now the day is over' was often sung! Those who reached Standard IV at the age of twelve were allowed to leave school. A few coppers were to be earned in fields in the evenings towards dusk. The farmers in those days were worried about the amount of sparrows and the harm they did, so a sparrow club was formed and some nets bought. The boys were paid one penny per dead bird. Older people say that sparrows' breasts were nice in a pie! The days of a farm worker before the First World War were very long. In summertime they worked from 4 am until at least 7 pm. The wives

Lacemaker 1890's

thought nothing of taking them food to the fields twice in a day. They were allowed the chunky pieces of wood when hedgecutting, so bought very little coal. Many of the women spent long hours in the harvest fields picking up the odd ears of wheat. Most of them kept chickens and were glad of the corn. Almost all the families had a pig or two in the sty and grew their own vegetables and fruit. On the very large allotment field, many had a little patch of corn sowed each year and a young man ploughed it for them for a small charge. There was one threshing day arranged in a barn near by and each one had his corn threshed and they each had their own flour ground for the year. All this seemed to stop around the First World War, and now the field is a patch of Council houses.

I.M. White, *Marsh Gibbon*

In 1917 I was born in the end farmhouse in Marsh Gibbon where I still live, so by now I really belong there.

We had a mile to walk to school and often arrived late as one attraction was the blacksmith's shop. We hung around the doorway for ages, watching the smithy and his son, clad in leather aprons, one working the large bellows and fire, the other shoeing the horses and moulding the iron work.

Next door to the blacksmith's was the butcher's shop and slaughter-house. On pig-killing days we rushed out of school at midday and whoever got to the butcher's first would claim the bladders. We blew them up and had great fun kicking them like footballs all the way home.

In a nearby field there were some very large pits twenty-five feet deep in places, from which the stones were dug and farm cottages built with them in the village a hundred years ago. People used to come from miles around to swim and fish here. It was here that I and many others learnt to swim in summer and skate in winter.

In the middle of the village is a very strong spring, Stump Well. The water is very soft, and brown with iron. The village was piped so that pressure would send the water to the end of the village and gravity would return it back through the village to provide for six taps. If luck was against you and someone at the farthest taps along the line was drawing water, you would wait for ages.

Our local doctor used nothing but this water to mix his medicines with. To him it was full of healing powers. The well is still here today but barricaded from humans and animals as it is in the middle of a field.

Near to the main road was a field with an open hovel in the centre. It was here that we achieved a tramp who became a permanent member of the village. Where he came from we never knew, or what his end was, but his stay was some thirty years. We called him Billy Wontwork.

Lydia Herring, *Marsh Gibbon*

At Marsh Gibbon there are wide grass verges on the sides of the roads. Before roads were tarred, the roadsides were wide to enable traffic to pull out of the ruts that formed in the middle of the road in wet weather. After tarring, these verges were used for grazing and making hay. Right up to the 1930's, at Marsh Gibbon the Parish Council auctioned them for the year. Small farmers were glad to pay £4 or £5 for a couple of miles of roadside where they then grazed cattle with an attendant or cut it for hay. In that village the money so made was given to the parish representative on the Rural District Council towards his expenses.

A great deal of milk went from Bucks on the Oxford-Bletchley railway line to Euston. The milk had to be at the station at 8 am—some thirty horses and carts converged on the station at Marsh Gibbon before the 1914-18 war.

The cows were all milked by hand and the milk all had to be run over a surface cooler before going to the station, and sometimes there was a dash to get there on time. The milk was on sale in Euston in the afternoon.

In frosty weather the pony had to be driven very carefully. The blacksmith would put longer nails in the horse's shoes to give a grip. These wore down quickly, and if the frost lasted more than six or seven days they would have to be done again.

Mr Batchelor remembers cutting corn with a scythe and then using a hook and a left-handed iron hook to make it into sheaves that were tied by hand with straw.

Later they had a 'Sailer', a two-horse drawn implement that cut the corn, which fell back onto the platform behind and some sails swung round and threw the corn loose in a sheaf onto the ground. This was tied by hand. Beans were not tied.

Later they had a binder drawn by three horses which cut and tied the sheaves. In the 1939-45 war one of these was converted to use with a tractor. Before it started in a field, one width had to be cut by hand all round so that it did not run over standing corn.

If the builder of a hay or corn rick was not very skilled the rick might lean and it would then have to be propped up with wooden stakes. These stakes were known as 'policemen'. A neighbour might comment, 'I see you've got a policeman up at your rick so's it won't run away'.

Quite a lot of hay was made for sale, much of it for the horses in London. This hay was 'trussed'. The trusser did this job throughout the year, moving his truss from farm to farm as required. He then used a knife to cut out slabs of hay. This was put in the trusser and a handle pulled down to press it tightly and tie string round.

Trussing was no longer necessary when hay was baled in the field in the 1940s.

Percy Batchelor (born 1895)

My home was in a huddle of houses surrounded by fields, except on one side where a canal and wide expanse of railway kept the town at bay. We had many more shops than most villages. Just over the canal bridge was the 'local', it was a good idea to give this a wide berth at turning-out time on Saturday night, or risk being bowled over by a lurching drunk. Opposite this was a power station, where gas was extracted from coal, turning it into coke.

Over the bridge was first a paper, tobacco and sweet shop. Next, a fish and chip shop where one could get 'a penny and pennorth'—a penny piece of fish and a scoop of potatoes, with vinegar and salt thrown in if wanted. A couple of houses separated that from the greengrocer's. Oranges cost four a penny, apples 1 or 2 lb a penny, according to the season, and a bag of mixed herbs (onions, carrots and turnips) only a few pence. At the grocer's shop there was rice, sugar, split peas, lentils etc. in sacks on the floor. These were sold in a wrapping of stiff blue paper screwed into a cone. On some occasions a rice pudding had to be skimmed before being put in the oven, or one got sacking hairs with it.

Next came the oil shop, where they sold fire-wood, candles, gas mantles, fire lighters and some hardware, besides paraffin.

Beyond the draper's shop about a dozen houses continued on, one of which was a barber's shop and had a striped pole standing out beside the door; and then, of all things, a coffee shop.

Across the other side of a cul-de-sac was a 'snob', or shoe-maker, and we were allowed to go in and watch him at his work, though he used to chase small boys away. He also renewed rubber heels, which were disks held in place by a screw. When worn at one edge, the disk could be turned, so that the worn edge was the other side of the shoe.

Quite a bit further down the road was another tobacco, sweet and paper shop where we could get 4 oz of sweet crumbs for a farthing. These were the bits of any kind of sweet left in the jars or boxes when they were otherwise empty.

Across another side road was a grocer's and off-licence. Here there were boxes of biscuits along the front of the counter with their tops off to show their contents. Then the 'milk shop' where they sold all kinds of dairy produce, and a very large earthenware bowl took up a good part of the counter. This was glazed, and white, with a picture of a cow in blue, with a sort of wreath of leaves round it. Customers took their own receptacle into which the milk was measured with one or half pint measures.

The last shop was a bakery, with lovely smells issuing.

A few more houses, then fields and more fields and on the nearest of these one of the first cottage homes for orphans was built.

In our nearest shopping centre was the Jubilee Clock, where on 'Hogmanay' Scotsmen, brought down to man the new McVitie & Price's factory, gathered to drink, dance and sing the old year out.

The baker brought our bread in a horse-drawn cart When he had gone by we looked up the road for manure, and if the horse had obliged ran out with bucket and shovel, for we had a small flower garden at the back of the house. Most people kept rabbits, chickens or pigeons.

48

Downstairs our house was gas lit, but we had to use candles upstairs. My brothers and father were all over six feet tall, so we had to keep a good supply of mantles in the house. The street was also gas lit, and at dusk the lamplighter came down the road carrying a cane with a hook at the end which he used to turn on the gas.

The milkman called round the village with a brass ornamental churn slung between two wheels. Horizontal bars held the measuring cans which were of a lead-like metal with flat brass hooks for the dual purpose of handles and to hold them on to the bar. We put lidded cans of the same lead-like metal on to the front step, and he filled them as he passed. The rag and bone man with his cry of 'Rag'ne a bone, bottle a bone', used a coster's barrow, as did the Hokey Pokey man who called 'Okey Pokey penny a lump'.

The canal came into my life. The playground of the infants' school overlooked it, with iron railings shutting it off. One teacher here would let us go out to watch the barges go by if we put our hands up in time. We always looked into the tiny cabin to see how much shining copper and brass they had, and often sparkling glass. Occasionally we would see a mirror framed in flowers painted on to the glass. The half door, and outer walls too, were usually brightly painted with all kinds of scenes and designs and the horses' harness shone with dangling brasses.

Anonymous, *Marsh Gibbon*

My great-uncle Rees Rees lived in Padbury one hundred years ago.

Rees Rees emigrated to Bucks from Wales, living for a little while at Piltch Farm, Adstock, before

Padbury

49

moving to become a tenant of All Soul's College, Oxford, at Manor Farm, Padbury.

At the age of seven my father, James James, came to live with him and luckily the housekeeper at Manor Farm was a kindly Welsh lady known to all as Margaret. It must have been very bewildering for a small boy to start life afresh and to learn a new language, as the only language he could speak was Welsh.

As he grew older he soon became immersed in the life at Manor Farm and under the tutelage of his uncle learned all about the ways of a dealer because that was the chief interest of Rees Rees.

Rees Rees purchased horses and cattle from small farms in Wales and these would be brought up by road to Padbury by drovers; incidentally, these drovers were put up at the New Inn at a charge of threepence per night but had to wash under the pump in the yard. The horses were unbroken and were shod by the Padbury blacksmith, Mr Sam Kirtland, and then were taken to the various horse fairs all over the country at Barnet, Stow-on-the-Wold, Banbury and Deddington.

Rees Rees did not have a bank account until he was quite an old man with failing eyesight, all the deals being made in gold sovereigns.

He was noted for his horses and was an accomplished driver. His ability to drive fast stood him in good stead when, in addition to farming at Padbury, he also became tenant of land at Stowe Park and on the Claydon Estate.

In those days none of the products of harvest were wasted, even the chaff being used with chopped mangolds to feed the cows. The mangolds were put through a machine which was turned by a handle. The cows were of course milked by hand in buildings surrounding the yard. After the milk had been strained, cooled and put into churns it was taken by horse-drawn float to Padbury station where it was put on the eight o'clock train to London.

The activities at the station were conducted under the watchful eye of the stationmaster, a notable character called Mr Ambler who was later to be presented by the residents with a gold watch for fifty years' service to the village. When the leading citizens of Padbury, Mr and Mrs Gore Langton from the Lodge, used the station on their journeys to London, on arrival in their resplendent carriage they were met by Mr Ambler who always wore a top hat on these occasions.

Rees Rees also brought sheep up from Wales. These were small and long tailed and were a constant source of friction among the neighbouring farmers as they could get through very small gaps in hedges. In early summer the sheep were taken to Thornborough Mill to be washed in the river, in order to enhance the value of the wool. Then came the sheepshearing which always took place in hot weather, it being easier to shear them when the grease from their body was present in the wool.

After shearing, the sheep were taken to a sheep dip situated by a pond adjoining some buildings called 'Dog Kennel' a little way down the Thornborough road.

The most important animals on the farm were the horses as they were involved in most of the activities.

Pig-killing days were events of importance. After the pig had been killed by a local slaughterer who journeyed round the various farms, it was immersed in a wooden tank filled with boiling water and all the hair was scraped off by means of an implement like a candlestick. The carcass was hung up for a day before being cut up into sides and hams, the immediate products being pork pies, faggots, brawn and chitterlings. The 'leaf' and spare fat were rendered down into lard. The bladder was eagerly sought after by the local boys as, blown up and dried, it made a splendid football. The main part of the pig and the hams were placed in leads in the cellar and were immersed in brine for some weeks before being hung up to dry.

51

Later, when I was living at Manor Farm, I found candle-making equipment up in the attic.

Margaret Crook, *Padbury*

In August 1924 I left Padbury School at the age of fourteen and started work at Manor Farm for Mr James James. I began as general odd job boy.

Hours at Manor Farm were from 7 am to 5 pm six days a week. My wages were seven shillings a week with any overtime at threepence an hour. For the first two weeks my mother let me keep the seven shillings to buy a pair of strong boots, for ten shillings. After this I gave my mother half my wages each week.

When the harvest was finished muck carting started, clearing all the muck from the yards to the fields. When this job was done ploughing began. I was then 'plough boy', driving a team of four horses for the ploughman. My ploughman, Jim Picketts, was a good-tempered man and I loved working with horses. We were at plough from 8.30 am to 2.15 pm with fifteen minutes lunch break. This was because Jim was also a milker.

With ploughing and drilling finished, the next job was mangold-pulling for winter feed for the cattle. When winter came I was set to work with the cowman, Will Salmons, who was a wonderful man with cows.

In my second year I was promoted to milk cart driver, and after my morning jobs round the cows were finished I was set to collect the eggs, clean the hen houses, get in wood and coal for the Missus and any other odd jobs around the house. Eventually I became a regular milker which meant starting at 6 am seven days a week, three hundred and sixty-five days a year as there were no paid holidays in those days. Still, even without holidays we were happy in our work.

I was a regular milker until I was eighteen and then I began to get annoyed when my mates were all dressed up on Sunday afternoons, so I left the farm.

Member's husband, *Padbury*

The village of Westbury, situated between the market towns of Brackley and Buckingham, saw a new squire installed just before Christmas 1902 when Sir Samuel Scott, MP for Marylebone, moved into Beachborough House. To celebrate the occasion Sir Samuel gave a house warming party for many of his friends which later became a regular event during the Christmas holiday when many of the inhabitants of the village helped in the house and at the table.

Although Westbury was quite small, it was a completely self-contained unit with its own abbattoir, butcher's shop, laundry and dairy, all of which provided work for the men and women of the village.

At the end of 1902 Sir Samuel Scott signed on Mr Steven Ward as his head cowman and Mr Ward, his wife and eight children moved from Brackley into

Westbury

53

Westbury where two tied cottages were knocked into one to provide a home large enough for ten people. The rent was one shilling a year, and the wage was sixteen shillings a week, plus as much separated milk as the family needed from the dairy at ½d a gallon. For sixpence the family could fill a large dinner plate with liver at the local butcher's shop.

At the age of nine years Mrs Bedden was taught the traditional art of Buckingham lace-making by Mrs Johnson, who was herself a maker of high-class lace. Mrs Bedden took her lace pillow and bobbins wherever she went, making lace for her own clothes and household trimmings and teaching her own daughter and grand-daughter. Lace parchments were made in the nearby village of Finmere by an old lady.

One of the most interesting commissions which Mrs Johnson received was to supply twelve lace table mats for an American client. These were despatched on completion, two at a time, for ten shillings each. The last pair crossed the Atlantic in the Titanic, and went to the bottom of the sea when this ship struck an iceberg. Eventually Mrs Johnson received compensation from the post office for the loss of her registered parcel.

In 1922 Mrs Bedden married and moved into the cottage in Westbury in which she still lives. In those days the rent and rates were 1s 8d a year and in 1974, still without mains water and drainage her rates are £23 a year. To fetch her water Mrs Bedden has to walk across the road to the village pump which is kept in use just for her.

The village had various events, most important of these were the May Day celebrations and the Westbury Feast.

On May Day the children were given the day off from school to dance the Maypole. The King and Queen, Prince and Princess, Duke and Duchess were chosen, and after dancing the children went in procession round the village carrying the May gar-

land. The garland was made from three sticks tied at the top, and joined to a hoop at the bottom. Two more hoops were placed in the centre to hold the May dolls, and the whole thing decorated with flowers and green foliage.

The other big date in the village calendar was the Westbury Feast which took place two weeks after Whitsun. This lasted from Sunday until the following Saturday. The main food was pork and ham as most households kept two pigs, killing one for the feast and selling the other to the local butcher. The money from the sale helped to buy two more weaners and food to keep them until the next feast. On the opening Sunday the ham was served to the friends and relations who came to the village. Other attractions were provided by two separate fairs, one in the playing fields, and the other in the Reindeer field.

Pauline Meads, *Westbury & Shalstone*

Miss Collins remembers the mill where her father worked before the First World War. It was powered mainly by water from the Ouse which drove the big wheel at the back end of the present building, and the present sluice was to divert surplus water. If water was short the machinery was powered by a steam boiler. The only lighting was tallow candles. The corn was first crushed by rollers, then ground on a stone wheel and finally brushed through fine silk stretched on revolving drums. In addition to fine flour the mill made semolina from the kernel of the wheat and the 'toppings' were made into bran and meal for pigs. Locust beans were also ground by millstones for cattle food. If Mr Collins wanted his dinner taken down to him, he signalled by stoking up the boiler to emit a puff of smoke—Miss Collins at a set time looked out of the back bedroom window to observe his signal!

At the top of the village there was another mill which made fertilisers from bones, rags, locust beans and other very smelly waste.

Lady Sophie Scott hunted, kept racehorses and entertained, and the Grafton Hunt met at the Lodge gates. The Scotts kept a fine herd of Jersey cows and one could get lovely butter and Jersey milk from the Manor.

They also installed main water, pumped from a spring in the spinney on the Billesden Road and the householders drew this water from standpipes in the street—there is still one outside the school—but before that all water came from wells.

Annually after Christmas the Scotts held a very grand Servants' Ball. Most of the guests were servants from the other great houses, but a few villagers who worked for the Manor were invited. Lady Sophie also gave an annual Christmas Party in the school for the children.

The District Nurse, Mrs Ernest Turner, a very popular figure, went around in a donkey cart. There was also Mr Law who lived in Brackley Road and made and repaired boots, a blacksmith and a butcher. 'The Barracks' were old thatched cottages on the site of Orchard Place.

The October Ox-Roast in Buckingham was a feature of their lives.

Alice Collins, *Westbury & Shalstone*

IV
Burnham
Hundred

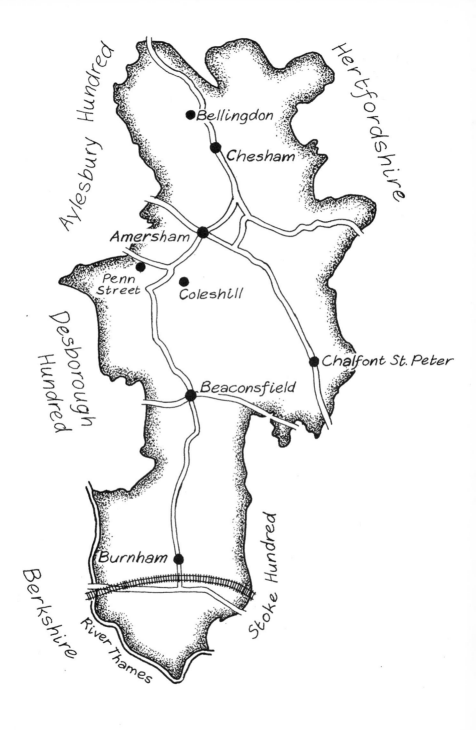

There were great times to be had when we were
young in Beaconsfield. Starting in May there was and
still is the annual fair which in those days was more in
keeping with the 'Olde English Faire'.

In addition to the roundabouts, gondolas, swings
and hooplas there were many sorts of merchandise
for sale. I remember a Mr Bell who came from High
Wycombe, a thin man with a moustache who always
wore a bowler hat, who pitched his stall in Windsor
End. His stalls were set in the form of a square and
were heaped to capacity with every conceivable piece
of china and crockery.

People from surrounding villages and hamlets
would wait for this day to refurbish their depleted
stocks of china and crockeryware. There were 'Willow
Pattern' tea and dinner services, white everyday
china-ware, blue and white striped jugs and many
other designs of varied colours and styles.

Mr Bell had children standing around spellbound,
for he would stack heaps of plates along his arm and
throw plates into the air and then catch them. He
drew large crowds and in the evening he auctioned his
wares until all his stock had vanished from his stalls.

We had in those days a school treat for the pupils
of Windsor End school. This was given by the
grandfather of the present Lord Burnham and was
held at Hall Barn. A carriage was sent to transport the
smaller children, and the older children marched in a
very orderly manner to Hall Barn. When they arrived

they would find that tea had been set beneath the trees by the Long Parlour, bread and butter, iced buns, macaroons, chocolate and plain swiss rolls.

After tea a man would play a whistle and bang a large drum to start the show. There was a 'Punch and Judy' and all kinds of great fun and we were given free ice cream cornets, served and made by an Italian from High Wycombe by the name of Mr Delnevo. This ice cream was made from corn-flour flavoured with essence of vanilla into a custard and then frozen. At the end of the day each child was given a bag of cherries and a currant bun by Lady Burnham.

The children, tired out from rolling down the slope in front of Hall Barn, were then collected by their parents and taken home.

If by chance the weather was wet then the treat was held in the coach-house.

On another day during the summer a Flower Show was held in Hall Barn Park. Three tents were erected, one for tea, one for flowers, and another for vegetables. There was very keen competition among the exhibitors of flowers and vegetables.

There were many competitions in progress, and a bowling competition for which the prize was a pig. Mr Beach had his roundabout there and the fares were collected by members of the Horticultural Society to help swell their funds.

Nora Croft, *Beaconsfield Old Town*

Bellingdon   Miss Emma Harding of Savecroft Farm, Bellingdon, near Chesham, writes of her grandparents Daniel and Emma Harding who told her of their childhood in the country. Daniel Harding was born in 1847. His grandfather was a farm bailiff at Ashley Green and was born in the latter part of the eighteenth century.

Daniel and Emma were married in July 1871. They walked to the church in Chesham for the wedding. Weddings were performed free to encourage couples to get married because so many people were living together.

When Emma Harding was a girl still at school, she got a job at a silk factory. She regretted it but her mother made her leave school to keep her promise to go to work. She had to get up in the dark and walk through unlit lanes to work.

Later she took a job nearer home, joining other girls and women in plaiting straw. These straws were first split with a little wooden implement and then plaited. The plaits were then taken to Luton to be made into straw boaters for men. This was a flourishing cottage industry around Chesham. A highly skilled worker could make sixty yards of 'three score' a day, but as the best price was a shilling a score or less she could hardly earn a pound in a seven day week.

5, 6, 7, 8 & 9 strand straw splitting tool

Both plaiters and lacemakers did without a fire because they had to keep the work clean, so they filled an earthenware pot with hot wood ashes and warmed their hands with it and sometimes they would put it under their skirts to warm their legs. These pots were called 'chaddy pots'. When the warm weather came they took the plaiting out of doors.

The corn was cut and tied by hand and there was one lady who cut and tied two sheaves of corn when she was a hundred and two years of age. A lot of the straw was taken to London to sell as there were many stables in London in those days.

The women and children picked up stones from the fields and these were placed in heaps by the roadside ready for road mending.

Once a week the huge brick oven was heated with furze, cut from the common, and faggots and when the oven was white hot all the cinders were removed.

61

A long wet mop cleaned the oven and then loaves of bread were gently laid in rows at the back of the oven using a wooden shovel called a 'peal'. Then at the mouth of the oven meat pies and cakes were placed. These lasted the family all the week.

Emma Harding (died Dec. 1973), D. Mills
Bellingdon & Asheridge

Chalfont St Peter The River Misbourne once flowed over the main road at one point and was known as 'the splash'. Horses and carts paused here to be washed down. When the first cars came they often got stuck in the splash and the local lads would call out, 'Push you out for a penny, Sir'. At times the houses were flooded and on one occasion the customers were marooned in a pub. A foot-bridge was built and eventually by 1968 the River Misbourne had competely disappeared under a shopping precinct and parking space with flats above.

The London to Aylesbury coach stopped every five miles and as a coaching stop Chalfont St Peter was a village of pubs. Several have been demolished in the last twenty years, but the Greyhound, visited once by Sir Winston Churchill on his way to Chequers from No 10 still stands. A few years ago a grand archway through which the coach and horses passed, was blocked up and made into a dining room.

When the first buses came, their route could be changed without warning because the driver went wherever the majority of passengers wished and stopped at their own front gates. The fare to London was half a crown.

There have always been gravel pits in the area, many now filled in and built on. A local pig farmer was distressed when because of swine fever his animals had to be destroyed, but while digging graves for them he found gravel and made more money than he ever had on pigs.

Phyllis Warden, *Chalfont St Peter*

Very little of the old village of Chalfont St Peter remains except the Church, the Greyhound Inn, and The Grange, now known as the Holy Cross Convent.

Amy Smythson, *Chalfont St Peter*

Village life in Coleshill has changed considerably since we were children about fifty years ago. It is a very beautiful village and over the past twenty years has attracted the financially better-off. Consequently all the cottages which in our childhood were rented to people with families, some of them quite large, have been bought up and enlarged and on the whole are occupied by elderly and retired people. Most of the young couples from the village are unable to afford to buy any property here—there being now very few to rent—so they have to move away to live, and this means that we have far fewer children living here.

Coleshill

As a village we are lucky in having our own school, church and Baptist chapel and quite a large hall, and fifty years ago our lives revolved mainly around these.

We had seasons for all our different games—of course, there was very little traffic about and so it was safe for children then to play on the roads.

In the spring we had our season for skipping to the rhythm of 'Salt, mustard, vinegar, pepper' and 'All in together, girls'.

We played with hoops—bowling them along the

road with a piece of stick—some of us couldn't afford a proper hoop and one wealthier family in the village gave us old car tyres which we used. Marbles was another game. We bowled them along the ground into a 'dossy-hole' made by screwing our heel round into the soft ground.

We derived great pleasure in picking bunches of wild flowers which grew everywhere; heather and harebells from the common, bluebells, primroses, cowslips, kingcups, milk-maids, fox-gloves, violets and celandines from the hedgerows. We also gathered many a basketful of dandelion heads for our grand-mother to make into wine and we picked baskets of blackberries in the autumn and collected wood each week to store for winter.

We were lucky in having our own village black-smith and wheel wright who used to allow a few of us at a time to go in and watch him at work, as did the village shoe mender.

There were two small shops in Coleshill which sold groceries and dozens of other odds and ends. We looked forward eagerly to our 'Saturday penny', which often we would spend a farthing at a time.

We used to visit the meadows in early spring to see the first lambs and in the early summer watch the sheep being sheared by hand and 'dipped'. At haytime and harvest we went into the fields to take the men's tea—usually sandwiches and a bottle of cold tea, always referred to as 'wittles' by my grandmother. A highlight on the farms in mid-winter was the visit of the threshing machine which travelled round the villages to thresh the grain from the sheaves of corn which had been stored in ricks since harvest.

Our local farmer brought the milk round in large churns by horse and cart—carried it to the doorstep in a large can with a half pint measure hanging on a ledge inside and served it into a jug. We could also fetch a quart jug of 'separated' (skimmed) milk for a penny for milk puddings.

More tradespeople came to the village then, such as grocers, butchers and bakers. On Good Friday our baker from Amersham would deliver warm cross-buns before we were up and leave them on the ledge above the door. The muffin-man came weekly through the winter carrying his tray of muffins on his head and ringing a hand bell. A traveller we called 'the London man' came down every Friday from London via Beaconsfield station with a huge case in which he carried an assortment of underclothes, socks and haberdashery for sale.

We never went on holiday but looked forward eagerly to our Chapel Sunday School outing—to Bricket Wood and Hampton Court and eventually to the seaside.

When anyone was seriously ill straw was spread on the road outside their home to lessen the noise of traffic—mostly horses and carts. There wasn't much hospital accommodation then. When anyone in the village died, the knell would be tolled by the church sexton—three 'strokes' for a man, two for a woman and one for a child. We all knew each other so well that if anyone was ill, and we heard the knell, we would realise straightaway who had died. This custom was dropped during the war.

Louie Edwards, Violet Darwill, *Penn Street (Evening)*

The little Church called St. Paul's, a Chapel of Ease, is about the only landmark which has not changed in any way, the same yew trees surround and shade it. Everything else is quite different.

The wood known as Eight Acres Wood at the far end of the field on which the church stands has been completely demolished. We always used to blackberry

Horn Hill

in this wood and get crabs for jelly, and the wood was a sheet of bluebells in the spring.

The cottage behind the village hall where I was born was very tiny and covered with pink roses. The orchard had several large cherry trees and the cherries were small and black and had an out-of-this-world sweetness. There was no water laid on in the cottage and my father used to go down to the bottom of the meadow nearest the road to the well, so we had to use water carefully. This well has disappeared. Also, under a holly bush half way between the church and the Dumb Bell, on the left side of the road at the end of Kiln Wood, was a spring, and water carts came to this for water when springs and wells were dry in other places. Although there is no actual pond as there used to be, the road nearby is never completely dry and springs of water can still be seen beside the road.

The postman used to walk from Chalfont St Peter to the pillar box near the Dumb Bell and would blow a whistle when he got to our corner, so that my mother could have her letters ready by the time he came down the road—and he also brought stamps and sold them to her.

The village hall was built in 1911 by Mr H. Harben, Chairman of the Prudential, who lived at Newlands Park, now a Teacher Training College, and it is on the site where there were five or six cottages on the corner.

Except for Braillings Lane, every other lane has been widened or altered and there is not one cottage or house unaltered, except perhaps the Crooked Billet and the Cross Keys next door. In this latter cottage my father was born one hundred years ago in November, 1874. Horn Hill Court, the 'big house', also cannot now be seen as it is a nudist colony and only the roof and upper windows are visible over high corrugated iron fences!

Mary E. Stevens, *Horn Hill*

V
Cottslowe Hundred

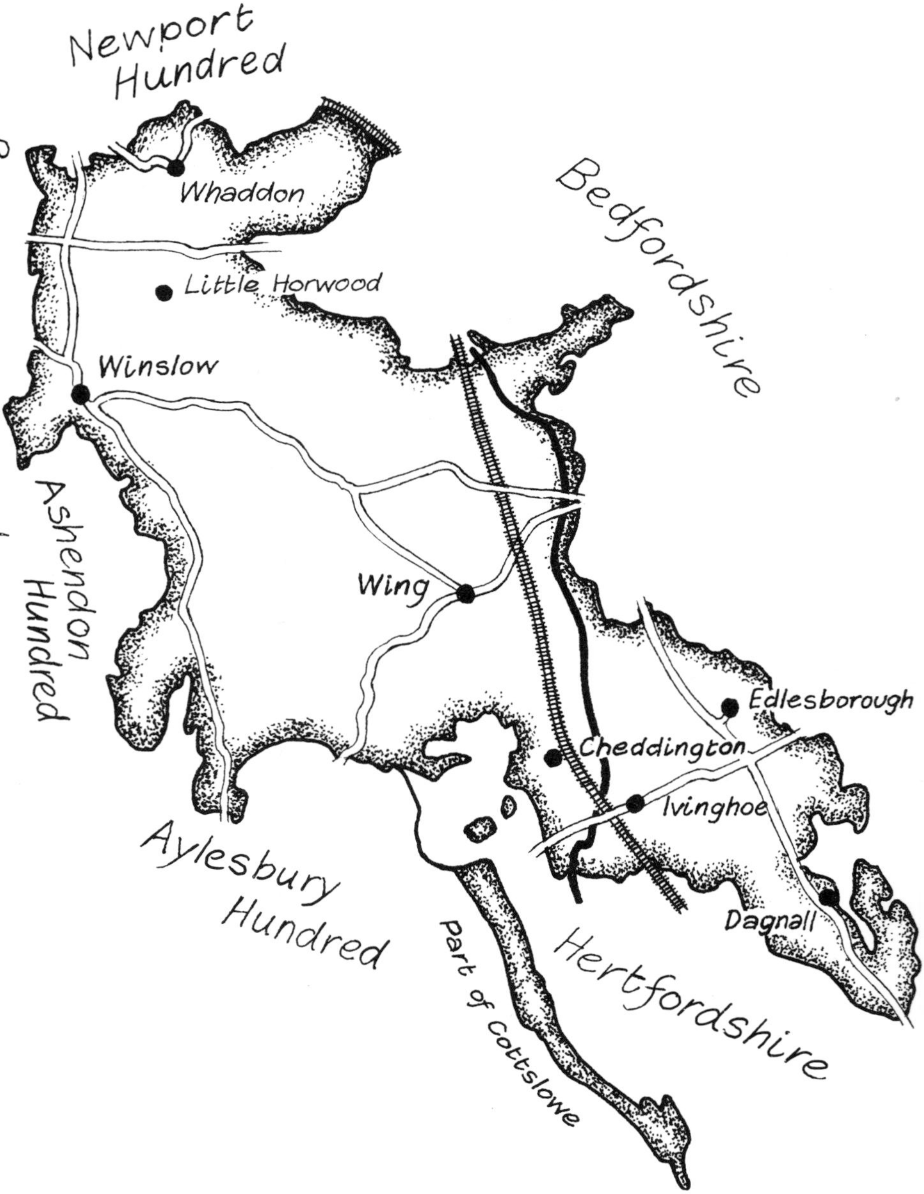

Newport Hundred

Buckingham Hundred

Bedfordshire

Whaddon

Little Horwood

Winslow

Ashendon Hundred

Wing

Edlesborough

Cheddington

Ivinghoe

Aylesbury Hundred

Dagnall

Part of Cottslowe

Hertfordshire

Local words

Hommocks along: walks in heavy boots with lumps
    of mud attached
Clapered: very dirty, muddy
Thragged: loaded
Sawny or *gallus*: stupid
Ceach: scoop of water
Sotchel along: walk along dragging the feet
Spraggle about: walk awkwardly
Lichup: lazy or walk slowly
Pottle measure: round measure for small apples,
    onions

Hare coursing used to take place regularly along the
Mentmore road and also pigeon and rook shooting.

Before a hearse came into common use, coffins
were placed on a wooden bier and pulled along the
Church Path to the church. The bier was kept in a
shed near the Church Lane allotments, along with a
bath chair for any parishioners in need of one.

Farmers used to go round the Lynces at night with
lights and nets to throw over the bushes to trap the
sparrows that did so much damage to crops. They
were paid so much for every sparrow caught and had
an annual Sparrow Club Dinner at Tring.

Dora McGuire, *Cheddington*

69

Dagnall   Dagnall was, and still is, one of the two hamlets in the
Parish of Edlesborough. The seven farms that sur-
rounded the village, together with nineteen cottages,
the Mission Church and the parsonage, belonged to
the Ashridge estate. Lord Brownlow was responsible
for the curate's living.

Edlesborough Church

All the properties situated between the allotment
gardens and the parsonage, and land stretching back
to the Studham Road, were owned by Messrs
Batchelor Brothers. Within the Batchelor's property
were a brewery, a malthouse, piggeries, and cottages
for those employed at the brewery. There was also a
small private chapel, as a result of some dispute with
the Methodists and the Church of England. The
Batchelors' private house was situated at the north-
west end of the village. Near the entrance gate was a
building called 'The Tramp Ward' that provided
shelter for one night for any tramp on his wanderings.
In the morning he was given a drink of small beer at
the brewery before continuing his journey.

Beer was also brewed at the Cross Keys public
house for sale in the house and for customers
requiring larger quantities in pins, firkins and larger
barrels. (Farmers provided beer for their men during
harvest, haymaking and threshing.)

There were three other public houses in the village,

but one, the Golden Rule, only had a six-day licence.

The main roads were little better than cart tracks, and tar roads were unknown until the early 1920's. The iron tyres of the farm carts would sink into the surface of the road to a depth of four or five inches. Footways on the roadside were in the centre of the grass verges and became very muddy during the winter months.

The doctor came from Dunstable, five miles away, sometimes on horseback, at other times in a brougham driven by a coachman. Medicines were dispensed by the doctor himself and left to be collected from an open window of his dispensary—often by someone travelling on foot to Dunstable.

The two bakeries in the village delivered to the door daily, as well as to neighbouring villages. Several butchers from other villages delivered to Dagnall in their traders' carts drawn by horse or pony. These carts were totally enclosed. Access to the goods was obtained by lowering the tailboard on chains, and the tailboard then became the cutting-up block. Spring balance scales hung from an arm extended from the top of the cart.

A four-wheeled horse trolley, laden with hardware, paraffin, candles and almost anything you cared to ask for, came round once a week. The draper brought his wares in a tilted cart, and from him mothers would buy yards of shirting to make shirts for their men folk.

Milk, however, was not delivered to the door for a good number of years. Skim milk was collected direct from the farm and cost about a halfpenny a pint. The cream from this milk was made into butter.

A sub-post office and general shop catered for most needs, and there was also a general shop attached to one of the public houses. The postman delivered the mail from Little Gaddesden, either by bicycle or on foot.

The mains water supply is comparatively recent.

Before its arrival drinking water had to be raised from the wells some fifty feet in depth. Rain water from the house roofs was stored in underground tanks and used for washing.

There was, of course, no main drainage, and toilets were usually situated at the far end of the garden. Sinks and drains discharged into dumb wells that allowed the water to soak into the chalk.

Dagnall School Church about the turn of the century

The Mission Church was a church on Sundays and a school during the week—until the new school opened on 11 January 1909. The single bell at the church summoned the congregation to worship and the boys and girls to school. One Sunday the churchwarden, who was very deaf, was tugging away at the bell-rope when the clanger parted company with the bell. Not being too sure if his hearing had deteriorated further, the churchwarden continued to ring. When the village blacksmith entered the church the churchwarden asked him if the bell was still ringing. The blacksmith shook his head, and the bell has remained silent until this day.

Written by Mr Putman, husband of Gladys Putman,
Dagnall

My father's family, the Seabrooks, were living in Ivinghoe in 1559 and we are the first names in the Church Register. I was born in 1893.

Mrs Henry Mann Roberts of The Brewery House was in charge of the Land Army in our district in 1917 with Headquarters at Town Farm where the girls were lodged.

One day Mrs Roberts called a meeting in the Town Hall, Ivinghoe, and brought with her to the meeting a Mrs Alfred Watt from Canada. Mrs Watt told us all about the Women's Institutes in Canada and explained how necessary it was for country and village women to help each other and make the best of the things they grew. After the meeting, Mrs Watt asked me if I would try and get the women of Ivinghoe, Pitstone and Ivinghoe Aston to form a Women's Institute at Ivinghoe. This was done in 1917 with great enthusiasm and I became the first Secretary. Unfortunately the minute books were lost and the present first minute book was written from memory by Mrs Roberts of Ivinghoe Manor who in 1919 became President, and remained so for about seventeen years.

We made rugs and carpets from wool called thrums, gloves, childrens clothes, knitted socks, and jams and pickles.

The WI subscription at that time was about 1s 6d, or 2s 6d per year. I am still a member.

Mrs Henry Mann Roberts also started a rug making class in the Town Hall, and her workers made a carpet for Queen Mary.

Straw plaiting was quite a big thing in Ivinghoe at that time, the women and even some men plaiting the straws or 'splints' into yards of material with which to make straw hats. When a score of plait was done, it was taken down to Sair Jane's cottage (Miss Sarah Jane Cook) who used to get it all ready for the hat manufacturers who came each week from Luton to buy the work. In the early days the women used to give their babies paregoric in water so that they would sleep for a long time and not disturb the plaiters.

Many of the men worked at Roberts & Wilson's Brewery next door to the church. The brewery was bought in 1927 by Benskins of Watford and closed and pulled down. The Brewery House is now a Youth Hostel with over eight thousand hostelers staying there each year.

Pitstone Hills

Other Ivinghoe men worked on farms, some of them having to walk right up to Ashridge to Lord Brownlow's lovely home. Houses were half-a-crown a week and wages from fifteen shillings a week upwards.

Our beautiful church had a set of very old hand bells and the Church Council lent them to the WI. Miss Marjorie Hartop taught us how to ring them and we had great fun ringing at Christmas parties for the WI and the Church. We had a lovely peal of bells ringing every Sunday. Now the tower is not safe so the bells can only be rung at the festivals.

Sir Bernard Miles often spoke of Ivinghoe in his King of the Chilterns series on TV as he once lived at Ivinghoo Aason as it was then called.

The old vicarage at Ivinghoe was once a coaching house.

74

At nearly eighty two my eyes are getting bad for writing, but in my opinion Ivinghoe and Pitstone WI, the oldest in Bucks, is one of the best run and most interesting Institutes in the country.

Madge Dollimore, *Ivinghoe & Pitstone*

Living in a small village and being the middle child of a family of seven, my childhood was very happy. We all had to work hard, but we had lots of fun too.

We all had to get up at the crack of dawn and were quite ready to go to bed early.

All our drinking water had to be fetched in buckets from a stand pipe in the street. We often had to take a kettle of boiling water to thaw the frozen tap in winter.

In the back yard we had a large covered tank and two tubs, which held the very valuable rain water.

Each Wednesday morning very early, all doors and windows were closed, and the village streets were deserted, for this was the day the sanitary cart came round. The wooden closets were right at the bottom of the garden, most of them had two seats, one for adults and a small one for children, so each closet had two buckets to be emptied.

We always kept two pigs in the sty, one for the house and one to sell. The profit made on the one sold, paid for the other.

It was a busy time when the pig was killed. There was all the offal to see to, and the lovely liver, and the fat of which some was always taken round to relatives and friends and then they returned the kindness when they had a pig killed. All the odd pieces of meat were made into big pork pies.

The chitterlings had to be thoroughly cleaned in strong salt water and had to be turned and put into

Little Horwood

At the bottom of the garden !

75

fresh salt water every day for a fortnight. The 'leaf', a large piece of fat, had to be cut into small pieces and put into a large saucepan and melted down to make great bowls of lard. The hard pieces that were left were called scratchings and were delicious with salt and bread.

The sides of bacon and hams were salted in a big 'lead', a large flat dish the size of a big table. Salt had to be rubbed into the meat for several weeks, then the sides of bacon and hams were wrapped in muslin cloth and hung in the kitchen to dry.

On Sunday morning two of us made the long journey right up the village to the bake house, one carrying a huge greased baking tin and large joint and the other a can of batter. Almost everyone in the village took their Sunday joint to be cooked like this. The Yorkshire pudding underneath the meat was just too good to describe.

In the spring we went at night time up the ridings to the edge of the woods to listen to the nightingales. On Good Friday everyone went to the woods to gather primroses to decorate the church and chapel and some for the home. The men spent the day on the allotments setting the early potatoes.

One of the year's loveliest days was May Day. My grandmother had a beautiful garden full of old-fashioned flowers. She used to pick a small bunch for the younger children and the older ones each had a Crown Imperial. We carried these flowers round from door to door singing as we went, all dressed up in our prettiest dresses, with daisy chains for hair bands, necklaces and bracelets.

May Day Song

'A May garland I have brought you
Before your door it stands
It's nothing but a sprout
But it's well spread about
By the work of the Good Lord's hands.

'Good morning Ladies and Gentlemen
We wish you happy May
We've come to show you our May garland
Because it is May Day.'

When anyone in the village died, the church bell was tolled at once and again before the funeral. All curtains and blinds were drawn over the cottage windows if the funeral procession had to pass by.

K.A. Savage, *Little Horwood*

I was born Maria Hopkins in 1889, the youngest of twelve children. There were many Hopkins in the village where ancestors had lived for at least four hundred years. My mother, aged eighteen in 1862, walked, in pattens, from Aylesbury carrying my brother, a babe in arms. We lived in a bungalow at Snelshall, where there was once a priory, for my father worked on a farm. At the age of five I started school at Whaddon, walking across the fields, unless the floods were out, when we had to go round by Tattenhoe. There were a hundred children in the school, built in 1841, a long building, divided into three. The infants' room had desks raised on a gallery where we sat all day. Mr Marshall, the headmaster, was strict but kind and my school days were happy. I left at fourteen. We were taught manners and the three R's. As my mother came from Stratton Audley she could not do Bucks lace so I went with other girls to Mrs Clark to learn, sitting round a stool with a candle and a bottle of water to reflect the light.

Two of my sisters died of diptheria in one week.

We never had a holiday, but went on Sunday School and Band of Hope outings in a 'brake'. I met my future husband, Sidney Meacham from Newton

Whaddon

Longville, on one of these excursions to Claydon House.

The first Christmas tree I saw at school was given by the lady at the 'Big House'. I was disappointed with the steel bead bag that was given to me!

I was a founder member of Whaddon WI in 1936.

A cousin was a hurdle maker and his son has his old tools with queer names like a 'frommer'.

Many words are no longer used. The fields—now joined together—had lovely names like 'The Pightle', 'The Big Fodderer', 'The Mutton', 'Hog's Piece' and 'The Canals'. Words connected with farming we used every day were *thave* (a sheep), *yealm* (a straw measure for thatching), *ennus* (hen house), *cow us* (cowshed), *yo*(eye), *housen* (plural of house), *tis-sacky* (poorly), *muckle* (manure), *hummocksing* (plodding), *thribble* (triplet lambs), *cherry cud* (a cow's first milk), a *boy chap* (big boy), *Grampy* (grandpa).

The corn and hay were cut with scythes and then tied by the binder; and we all went gleaning to feed our hens. We took Dad's 'baver' to the field to him, probably a Buckinghamshire clanger (a suet roll with bacon at one end and jam at the other) with home made beer.

Maria Meacham (a founder member), *Whaddon*

VI
Desborough
Hundred

Oxfordshire

Aylesbury Hundred

Saunderton

Radnage

Stokenchurch

Studley Green

Bradenham

Naphill

Burnham Hundred

High Wycombe

Lane End

Flackwell Heath

Bovingdon Green

Hambleden

Great Marlow

River Thames

Medmenham

Berkshire

I came to live in Bovingdon Green in 1906, when my father went to work as head gardener at a large house called The Orchards, where they kept a carriage and a pair of lovely black horses. I was five years old at the time.

I went to Bovingdon Green village school where there were about eighty children with three teachers. It sounds quite a large school for such a small village, but families were big in those days; there were six children in my family and thirteen in another! Children used to come from outlying farms and cottages, some of them walking three to four miles each way. After the first war, the school was closed and the building unfortunately knocked down. A private house called School House, which still exists, was built on the site. The iron railings that surrounded the original school remain round the house.

There were about fifteen cottages around the village green and two pubs. The first one, the Royal Oak, beside the village pond, is still there and has not changed very much. At the other side of the green was the Jolly Cricketers which had a pretty garden where people sat sipping their drinks in the summertime. Parties used to travel out from London for the day in horse-brakes, bringing their food with them for what they called a 'bean-feast', which they washed down with beer from the Jolly Cricketers. I can remember them throwing pennies to us children which we hastened to spend at a cottage on the green,

81

where the wife sold sweets which she produced from jars kept under her bed. They were 4 oz for one penny!

The Jolly Cricketers was later closed and became the village shop with a little post-office. This has now also gone. When I was a child there was no shop in the village, so if we wanted to visit the shops we walked the two miles into Marlow. But there was no need for this really as the baker, grocer and butcher called every day; also paraffin was brought to the door.

On Empire Day, 24 May, we danced round the Maypole on Bovingdon Green dressed in our white frocks, with the boys in white blazers.

I left school at fourteen and went to work at The Orchards. There were three gardeners and four staff in the house. I started in the kitchen and after some time was housemaid, parlourmaid and finished up as cook. We had plenty of work to do but were quite happy.

Jerome K. Jerome, who wrote *Three Men in a Boat*, lived in a house on Marlow Common, which is just beyond Bovingdon Green. I can remember going to tea at his house with my brothers and sisters.

Elsie Frith, *Bovingdon Green*

My parents married in the early 1920's and bought a bungalow on the Frieth Road between Marlow and Frieth.

There was a post box not far from our home. If my mother had no stamp, she put letter and stamp-money into a paper bag before posting the letter in the box. The postman then bought the stamp and stuck it on. At that time he did a long country round by bicycle, but previously he delivered and collected on foot, using the footpaths as the flint roads were too hard on a bicycle.

One summer the wild strawberries were particularly abundant and large. We picked several pounds of them and my mother made wild strawberry jam. It had a flavour all of its own.

Leslie Piercey, *Sands*

I was born, as was my mother before me, at the Bradenham Red Lion. My grandmother died when my mother was eighteen years old so she and my grandfather ran the pub until he died and then my father took it over.

Bradenham is now a National Trust Village but before that it was preserved as an old Manor holding by the Graves family.

The Graves family were very domineering folk. The Reverend Graves was strict with the villagers about attending church on Sundays and woe betide any parishioner who failed to turn up for service. When he died, his son had the living; at his death his widow had a life interest. Her maiden name was Tempest and she reverted to that as widow after the death of her two brothers in the 1914-18 War, which made her the last of her line. Mrs Tempest vigorously opposed any change in the village and it is consequently much the same as in its feudal days. Only recently has one house been erected—the first in over a hundred years. She lost the battle with the Air Ministry, however, and land on the outskirts of the village was compulsorily purchased in May 1940, to build what was then Bomber Command Headquarters. She did force through certain provisions, principally that no buildings or overhead wires were to intrude on the line of the Queen's Ride which was a path cut through the woods and countryside for the use of Queen Elizabeth I when she came to visit the Manor.

Another old house on the Common is Admiral Silver's House. After the death of Miss Silver, the last of that line, the Hudson family from West Wycombe rented the property from The National Trust and made it into the very beautiful house it is today. They were carvers by profession and in addition to carvings in the house made the lovely interior door of St. Botolph's church. The church is separated only by a wall from the old Elizabethan Manor House.

When I was young Mr Ball, the blacksmith, was also the verger of the church.

Bradenham held the prettiest Garland Day for miles around on May Day. The garland of fresh flowers was always made by Mrs Brown, the wife of the Keeper of the Woods, who only earned £1 a week to keep a wife and family of seven children. On Garland Day, all the children wore their most colourful clothes and after the May Revels went out singing, first to the Manor House and then to the workhouse at Saunderton. We also danced around a Maypole at the fete held in the Manor grounds every summer.

Dora Smith, *Sands*

Flackwell Heath

I was born sixth in a family of nine in a cottage on the farm where my father worked. There were six fields belonging to the farmer and all were named. There was Home Meadow, Half Yarch, Long Close, Pond Field, Leg of Mutton Field and Six Acres, each describing the shape, size or situation.

84

I started school when I was four years old at the Infant School in Flackwell Heath. We used to gather blackberries for the war effort to be made into jam or dyes. Later I moved from the Infant School down to Wooburn Church of England School and this meant a walk of over two miles through fields and woods or three miles by the road. During the war and for sometime after we could go to the Welcome Hotel which was just opposite the school, and for one halfpenny we were given a bowl of lentil soup and a piece of bread. This was subsidised by the nearby mill owners, Mr Thomas and Mr Green.

We used to pick Bee orchids and Fly orchids on the golf links, and sainfoin, scabious, blue chicory and knapweed in the fields and listen to the linnet, Jenny Wren and Writing Schoolmaster (yellowhammer).

Anne Allen, *Wooburn*

My father owned the village shop, which meant that he was grocer, butcher, baker, draper and also had carriages—a brougham, victoria, landau and wagonette for hire. The village was two miles from the station so there was quite a bit of station work to be done and elderly ladies to be taken to church and out visiting. There were very few cars about. The doctor had one of the first, a De Dion-Bouton, to replace the high dogcart he had always driven previously. When I was seven, my father was very ill with double pneumonia and that meant a daily trudge to the squire's house for ice to bring down his temperature. In the corner of a meadow near the head gardener's house was a round wooden hut, thickly thatched almost to the ground. Inside was quite a deep pit which, during the winter when the various lakes in the park became frozen, was filled up with big blocks of ice where they remained frozen right through the summer. The winters were very much colder then and there was always ice to be had from the 'ice house' and we used to love to go into the chilly darkness and watch Mr Swanborough chip off big pieces of ice with a clean garden spade. We then wrapped the ice in flannel and carried it home in a fish basket.

In the spring-time there was primrosing. We knew every bank and hedge row where the best ones were to be found, where the red oxlip grew every year and where, among the cowslips and milkmaids which grew in a low-lying meadow, we would find numbers of early purple orchids. A little later there were afternoons by the river where we gathered king-cups and Lodden lilies.

During the winter we killed three pigs every week and there were chilly afternoons spent in the cold damp slaughterhouse helping to make the sausages. There were the long strips of fat and the 'flays' to be cut up and cooked in the copper to make wonderful home-made lard. The next night the copper would be in use again to heat the water for our weekly bath in front of the kitchen fire.

Down the road was the big village pond which was often frozen over in winter hard enough for skating and sliding and where in the summer horses and carts drove in at one end to let the horses cool their legs and get a drink and drive out the other end.

E.M. Wootton, *Flackwell Heath (Afternoon)*

Hambleden

A neighbour, aged eighty-seven, who has lived in Hambleden all his life, tells me that when he was fourteen years of age he worked as gardener's boy at the Rectory. He disliked most the days when he had to 'Go Tag'. This meant that he was roped to the front of the lawnmower which he had to pull across the very large lawns, while it was guided by a more senior gardener.

R.T. Landragin, *Hambleden*

I was born in 1877 and have lived in or around Hambleden since I was a child and am now retired and living at Mill End, Hambleden.

As a small girl I lived at Aston Ferry and I remember when the River Thames was completely frozen over and a waggon and horses was driven over the ice and up New Street, Henley. My father skated from Aston to his work at Greenlands, roughly a couple of miles up river to the Bucks side of Aston Ferry (now Hambleden Place) and an extra horse was fetched from Mill End Farm to pull the waggons up to the farms at Rotten Row and on to Frieth.

The barge 'Maid of the Mill' used to leave Hambleden Mill once a week to take the flour to Huntley and Palmers at Reading, and she used to return on Friday loaded with broken biscuits that were sold to the local inhabitants for about one shilling for three pounds.

Laurie Woodford (96 in 1973), *Hambleden*

Sixty-two years ago I came from London and noticed the extremes of town and country life very keenly.

We cooked on a kitchen range that had to be cleaned with black lead, with a fender and fire-irons of steel. We had an oil lamp to light the evenings and we used a candle to light us to bed, not forgetting the hurricane lamp to light us to the outside toilet, which was of the bucket type. There was no main water supply, no sewage, or electricity.

Washing day was extremely tiring, all water having to be pumped. It took twenty six pumps to fill one bucket. Fifty buckets were needed to fill the copper.

The men folk worked equally hard. They worked from 7 am until 5 pm and those who worked with animals did extra duty on Saturdays and Sundays without extra pay, making for many men a seven day week of work. They grew all-the-year-round vegetables to supplement rations for the family. The husbands' wages were generally between thirty shillings and two pounds a week. A cottage was provided rent free with exception of a small contribution towards the rates.

Crafts such as basket making, lace making, and chair caning, were carried on by many housewives in their spare time, to earn money to provide clothes for the children.

In the early years barges drawn by horses carried loads of timber, coal and other goods along the river. The towpath was on one side of the river only, but changed sides at Aston Ferry. This necessitated taking the horse across the river at this point by ferry. At that time the towpath passed in front of Hambleden Place.

Foot passengers crossed by boat and the attention of the ferryman was called by ringing a bell. The fare was one penny per journey and the boat was large enough to carry several passengers and a bicycle or pram.

A coach called 'The Venture' owned by a Mr Brown of Henley ran at weekends from Hambleden to Reading. It was an open coach with a canvas hood and it was considered very modern to travel by it.

A carrier also served the village of Hambleden and

the surrounding area. He was a friend to all, calling several times a week, and would take two or three passengers at a moderate fare to Henley Station. He took orders from housewives for goods from shops and would bring them on his next trip. He also transported all kinds of produce and luggage to the station.

About fifty years ago an enterprising man started a bus service from Marlow to Henley. It was a single decker with a driver only. The fare to Henley from Mill End was 4d, from Greenlands 3d and from Fawley Big Oak 2d single. After a few years the Thames Valley Bus Co. took over this service.

In the early Thirties main water was taken to the village. Until then the pump in the village served many cottages with water and in early mornings a queue of waiting folks was the usual sight. Electricity followed a few years later but main drainage did not reach Hambleden until 1957.

The first historical mention of a mill at Hambleden was in the Domesday Book of 1086, when the mill and the surrounding land including Marlow was given to Queen Matilda by the Norman King William. The mill itself was then worth twenty shillings and the King exacted an annual tax of one thousand eels from its adjoining fisheries. The flour mill itself stopped working some years ago but much old machinery is still to be found inside.

In 1912 a Roman Villa was excavated not far from the present Car Park in Hambleden Road.

These are my memories of over fifty years ago.

Louisa M. Bramhead, *Hambleden*

I was born at High Wycombe and until I was about eight we lived at Vine Cottage on London Road. I remember being taken by my parents to my father's office, which was on the main road near Sweetlands, the photographer, to wave a Union Jack and to watch the procession celebrating the coronation of King George V.

I attended Sunday School in a little chapel on the main road towards Loudwater; a bridge went over the stream leading to it.

We used to walk to Keep Hill, the Rye and the Duke, across the fields over a stream near a public house to Loudwater village, to a viaduct on the London Road near which was in later years the Transport Garage. This viaduct sent back a marvellous echo.

An uncle always took me to a sweetshop in White Hart Street to buy chocolate butterflies.

My grandfather lived in the Queen's Head, Frogmore and the Orange Tree public houses during part of his lifetime; he also had a greengrocer's shop. We visited various friends and relatives, among them were Mrs Busby at the Railway Arms, Bristows the Chemist in Crendon Street, Worleys the Carriers where the smell of horses, hay and furniture were outstanding, Nurse Drake who lived somewhere along the London Road opposite the Rye, and an old lady who lived in an almshouse opposite the Technical School—a cake was always taken to her.

On Sunday mornings fresh-picked mushrooms were brought to people's houses, for sale, so that mushrooms were always a Sunday breakfast treat.

One Christmas we spent with relatives who lived in Hughenden Road. My father and uncle went along with a sucking pig in the baking tin to the local baker who cooked it and we collected it later.

C. Smith, *Denham (Afternoon)*

90

The road between Peacock and Cadmore End was very quiet in 1935, it being quite an event if a bicycle passed that way.

Memories of the Lacey Farm at Bolter End, and the use of horses and carts. The carthorses and long wagons piled high with sheaves of corn to be stored in barns and later threshed—no combine harvesters in those days. A very dirty job the farmer faced when the threshing machine visited his farm. Hay was all carted and made into ricks, something which is almost a thing of the past in this part of the world.

Milk was delivered by Joe Figg, who carried a large can and walked on his round delivering in the neighbourhood.

Cattle were grazed on the commons—cows and sheep too. Since the cattle have ceased to graze on the commons, a tractor mower has had to be employed to cut the grass.

Later came buses, memories of Hollands, who first ran a huge lorry into High Wycombe from Lane End. Mr Tom Ashby ran a small brown bus which was always full to capacity. His wife travelled with him and took the fares. Tom always waited for his regulars if they were a bit late!

Men journeyed into High Wycombe chiefly on bicycles from the surrounding villages, working long hours in the chair factories with one week's holiday a year unpaid.

Warren's old shop in the High Street sold everything in the grocery line and hardware. Goodchild's shop (now Sunset Stores) was another landmark of the village, in those years run by Bert and Fred Goodchild. Always plenty of sweets to be had there for ½d or 1d. Mr Fred Bates had his own bakehouse (now Crockett's Dairy) at Bolter End. His hot cross-buns were delivered piping hot on Good Friday morning in time for breakfast. Mr Arthur Plumridge also baked and delivered assorted cakes from a bakehouse behind the old post office.

There were no houses in the Cressex area forty years ago, except about two. The land at the top of Marlow Hill was all fields, and part was used by the Technical School as playing fields adjoining the lacrosse pitch belonging to Wycombe Abbey School.

Beryl Free, *Lane End*

Seventy-six years ago our village could have been called the village of the five ends as it consisted of the main village of Lane End joined by the hamlets of Wheeler End, Cadmore End, Bolter End and Moor End. These were only short distances from the Parish Church in Lane End. There were only two main roads in the village, one from Stokenchurch to Marlow, the other from Wheeler End to Frieth. Most of the houses were built on or around the commons and approached by footpaths. There were seven pubs named after the work done in and around the village—for example, the Chairmakers (now the Victoria) and the Old Armchair; or the Brickmakers at Wheeler End that backed on to the old claypits, and the Old Kiln which is now a house. There was also a very old pub in Stonor named the Broad Arrow, that had once been the home of some fletchers who made very good arrows. All these pubs were, more accurately, beer houses and were known locally as 'jerry houses', allegedly for the obvious reason.

There was no piped water—though there were many ponds where horses were taken for a drink. Each house had its own rain water tank in the garden and a barrel to collect water for washing purposes. Both supplies depended on the rain collected from the roofs. During a drought water was obtained from land springs and people used a yoke and two buckets to fetch the water. Most of the shops were in Lane

End near the main road. There was a butcher, baker, grocer, shoe mender and a general shop which sold everything from pins to oil, braces, mending wool. All houses and shops were lit by oil lamps.

Sunday was strictly observed. People either attended the church or the Wesleyan chapel—all dressed in their Sunday best with shoes neatly polished. There were two schools built at opposite ends of the village by the two churches and known as the Church and the Wesleyan schools. Most parents took their children for walks through the fields or woods on fine Sunday afternoons. It was very rough and dusty walking along the roads which were made from flints thrown down and then pressed into the ground by a steam roller after water had been thrown on them. Shoe leather didn't last long in these circumstances.

The only public transport was the carrier's cart. In Lane End there were two carriers who took people to High Wycombe three or four times a week at a cost of sixpence or eightpence for the return journey. Passengers often had to walk up the hills to assist the horse. With the exception of the Penny Farthing no bicycles were seen.

Men known as chair bodgers worked in the beech woods in sheds and, using a foot lathe, turned chair legs. The wood chips from these were collected into bags and sold locally by the 'Chip' man at fourpence a bag. Other local employment was provided by a brickyard, an iron foundry and a blacksmith and by the steam factory that made boxes for tin plate and chairs.

On weekdays the women wore shawls and white starched aprons. Men wore bowler hats on Sunday and caps on weekdays. Girls wore white starched pinafores, black stockings and boots. Boys were dressed as girls until they were five years old. Then they wore jackets with wide lace collars and wide brimmed hats with elastic under the chin. Most women and girls did lace making on pillows. Some did beautiful work and one Lane End woman received a gold medal for her lace at an exhibition in London.

Once a muffin-man appeared from High Wycombe and rang his bell around the village. Many of the poor families worked in the fields picking up stones and filling buckets with them. Heaps of these were later broken by a stone-breaker and used for road making and other things. May Day was always celebrated in the village with garlands and Jack-in-the-Green boughs. Dancing round the Maypole was also done. Lane End was proud of its local brass band with their uniform of scarlet and gold braid.

In 1897, when Queen Victoria celebrated her Diamond Jubilee, all the children were given a tea in Mr Slocock's barn at the Moor Farm.

R.E. Bristow, *Lane End*

I was born in 1892 and lived at Lane End, five miles from High Wycombe, and was the third daughter in a family of eight.

My father was a bricklayer, and when there was no work through bad weather, there was no money and my mother had to supplement the family income by lace making and caning chairs. Later she taught me to make lace. My sister and I walked to North's Chair Factory at Piddington, two miles away, before school, to collect the chair seats or frames, and two sorts of canes and wood for pegging. My mother did them during the day and after school we walked again to the factory, taking the completed caned chairs and collecting more to be done the next day.

I left school at the age of thirteen having obtained the necessary number of attendance marks and went into Service to live in at a house near Aylesbury. I was taken by horse and trap with my tin trunk and will never forget those first days away from home.

F.M. Woodstock, *Beaconsfield Old Town*

River Thames at Marlow

I come of a bell-ringing family. My grandfather, who was manager of the rope wharf opposite the 'Compleat Angler' (where now Turk's Boat Yard is) pealed the bells for forty-five years. In those days the ringers used to spin their own 'string' for the bells and would go to the rope wharf to do it, where there was space for the ropes to be laid out. Grandfather was also elected verger of the church in spite of his refusal to bow and scrape to any odd Lord or Lady who chose to walk through the churchyard.

Marlow

We went to the Parish Church four times on Sundays. After the last service, we walked round Westhorpe Park, now lost under the motorway, and had our weekly treat of ginger pop. In 1897 the spire of the church was struck by lightning and the steeplejacks were called in to repair it. A little unwisely, they left the ladder up and in the evening my cousin, Mary Truss, clambered to the top. The vicar was furious, the Truss's landlord (they kept the

Two Brewers inn) threatened to evict them: but it all ended happily with the steeplejacks presenting the daring Mary with a gold watch.

Once a friend and I walked along the river to Bisham side and to Sandy Bay. At the second bridge, General Sir George Higgison was passing underneath in his boat and called out, asking where we had been. When we said 'to church', he gave us twopence each. I kept that twopence for years but finally succumbed to the temptations of a local sweets' shop. The General lived to be a hundred years old and gave Marlow the land now known as Higgison Park.

The big event of the year was Marlow Regatta. The original Maidenhead and Marlow Rowing Club was formed in 1871 with a subscription of half a guinea per annum and donors of ten guineas were made life members. For two guineas you could become a vice-president. Eleven years after that Marlow ran its own regatta and gradually it became the largest open competition of its kind in the world.

Another big day was Rag Regatta when they hung tyres from Marlow Bridge and the contestants in punts had to climb through them. They also played water football and the entire river bank was open to watchers and no enclosures allowed in my young days.

May Harvey, *Sands*

Medmenham My parents and I came to Buckinghamshire in 1921. On our way we observed four cottages. In large white-washed lettering were the words 'I BE TO LET', on the next cottage 'SO BE I', on the next 'I BAIN'T' and on the fourth cottage, 'NOR BAIN'T I'. We thought this highly amusing, but as time went on we found this was typical Buckinghamshire dialect. At school I could not understand when there were arguments amongst the children, some would say 'Letter B', meaning 'Let 'er be'.

For many years there was a bib factory in Marlow. Round about 1917 there was a fire which damaged the factory but all who worked there managed to carry on, including my husband's cousin Bella who used to make bibs for twopence a dozen. There were bibs for the rich and bibs for the poor, the best bibs were made of silk and satin and were made for sixpence a dozen.

In 1925 my mother joined Medmenham WI where she learnt to make her own soap and to cure rabbit skins. When the skins were completed they were made into gloves for my sister and me.

Mary Mitchell, *Medmenham*

Naphill

There were eight in my family, four boys and four girls, and we lived in a tiny cottage at Naphill. There was no piped water and if it was a dry summer and the water failed, we had to fetch it with a yoke and buckets from the farm.

My father was a brick-maker and was often up day and night firing and baking the bricks. When this happened, we children took his meals to him and sometimes he built a little brick oven out in the open where we cooked potatoes, sitting around eating them with him.

My uncle 'Pudgy' Parslow kept the Black Lion, a sawdust and spittoon local pub. Another uncle and aunt had a farm at Walter's Ash where the whole Parslow family gathered at Christmas and anything up to forty people could be present.

We went to a Church of England school which is still there but now used as a church. We went to church three times on Sundays, changing out of our best clothes in between services. On Empire Day, our school competed with Cryer's Hill school for a shield. On Prize Day, Mrs Coningsby-Disraeli always gave the needlework prize, a lovely sewing basket. I never won it.

The big event of the year was the Naphill Flower Show in August and it is still the big thing in the village.

Daisy Aldridge, *Sands*

My father was a chair-maker and cycled each day to Wycombe to work. He was the drummer in Naphill band. I helped him carry the drum while the band was marching and not playing. The band played for concerts and children's Sunday School treats. On practice nights during the summer, they all sat round in a ring in my grandparents' garden and played—such a lovely sound that often attracted nightingales.

My mother had lived at Vincent Farm, next to the blacksmiths. The farm was owned by the Disraeli family who used to visit my grandmother.

Our lavatory was outside. It had a wooden seat, with squares of newspaper and a bucket underneath which was emptied once a week.

In our home we had no electricity but oil lamps for downstairs and candles to go to bed. The bed was an iron frame with brass knobs and a feather bed to lay on. We had a bedroom each, but in my father's time there were only two rooms for mother, father and seven children.

My mother used to wind my hair around long pieces of white rag and I slept in these and in the morning I had long curls.

My mother could make pillow lace, and each year most mothers made cherry pies. These were really lovely.

Naphill was famous for its bricks. The men dug for clay during winter, making very big holes. Very big sand-stones were also dug out and these were split and used for curb stones. In the summer, bricks were made from the red clay. They were stacked to dry and then put in the kilns.

Gladys Woodrow, *Sands*

Eighty years ago the village had two blacksmiths, three wheelwrights, three undertakers, two bakers, two shoe repairers, two butchers, and a tailor. We were independent of mains water as each house had a tank where rain water was stored. There was a village well, and springs nearby which were used in dry weather. There was also a sort of mobile cistern where villagers could buy a pail of water for one penny. Well water was very chalky and had to stand some time before being used. There was no gas or electricity.

Stokenchurch

Women sat at their front doors, with a bundle of canes hanging from a nail, caning chairs for which they were paid twopence a chair. Rushes were brought from Shubbington and Shillingford for matting chairs. They had to be soaked in water, usually the pond, and used the next day. Lace was also made in the doorways on fine days and evenings. A craft which has died out in the village was tambour beading: one lady employed five girls at one time.

There was a communal drying green where ropes were attached to a pole in the centre and the other ends tied to a tree.

The stage coach ran from London to Oxford. Two

99

horses in the village were used to meet the coach at the foot of old Dashwood Hill (the present cutting was made in 1926), hitched to it and helped pull it up the hill. They performed the same service at the foot of Aston Hill on the return journey. The bottom of Dashwood Hill was said to be a haunt of Dick Turpin, and he is reputed to have lived in the village at one time.

The blacksmiths, Bill and Bert Barney, were local characters and their garden was entirely edged with up-turned Bovril bottles.

Sunday dinner could be cooked by the bakers. One dish cost one penny, but potatoes, batter pudding and meat cost a penny ha'penny. Up to forty years ago, food could be taken and cooked specially if one was entertaining for a large number of people. Dough could also be bought, the customer's own bits and pieces added and taken back to be baked.

The employers of the chairmakers kept truck shops where groceries and clothes were sold and the workers were expected to spend part of their wages there. Lace-making cotton was also sold.

At the end of the Boer War when the men who had been fighting came home, their horse-drawn cart was met on the outskirts of the village at the Raven, the horses unhitched and the men of the village drew them home to the cheers and welcome of their families and friends.

The village had two brass bands, the Stokenchurch Temperance Band and the village band. A German band used to visit once a month on a Monday, and play at various points around the village. They did not return after the war.

Another event was the Annual Horse Fair. During the day horses were run singly or in pairs up and down the street to show off their paces to prospective buyers.

There used to be a windmill where villagers could take their grain and have it ground. Only the name

Mill Lane remains as the mill was blown down during a gale.

The village had a lock-up where rowdies were kept overnight and usually let out next morning or taken to the court at Watlington.

Members of *Stokenchurch*

My early life was spent at Hill Farm, near Stokenchurch near the top of Aston Hill. The farm was a 'clearing' of about one hundred acres cut out of the woodland and had been a bulb and flower farm. The land was cleared of bulbs but a few escaped and to this day a few wild daffodils grow in the boundary hedgerows. For many years some white narcissi grew in a pit in the middle of the field. In the paddock behind the cottage grew bright red anemones which defied all cultivations. There were large orchards surrounded by lilac bushes. Under the trees grew masses of Mahonia Aquifolia which we used to call Berberis. The leaves of these were packed with the flowers when they were sent to market.

We had two plough teams of beautiful shire horses. The ploughman's day began very early as the horses had to be fed and watered before they went into the field, and there was only a very short break for the mid-day meal. The horses had a nosebag of chaff and oats, the men had a 'thumb piece', a lump of bread about an inch thick with a large lump of cheese or very fat home-cured bacon. This was held between thumb and finger and cut with a pocket knife, washed down with a bottle of cold tea or wine mixed with water. The men rarely sat down to eat but just rested on one knee. Ploughing finished for the day about three o'clock and the horses were fed, watered and groomed before the ploughman could have his own tea.

Water was a great problem during the summer. We had a pond on the farm but as we had about twenty milking cows, each drinking ten gallons of water, the pond soon dried up. We had three underground fresh water tanks, collecting water from the roof of house and buildings for household use, but this often ran dry as well. Water was collected in a horse-drawn water barrel from Swilley pond in Stokenchurch for the cattle and drinking water from the village well.

During the very dry summer of 1921 all the ponds dried up. The water for livestock was fetched by water barrel from Nethercote about five miles away. This meant continuous shifts of water-cart day and night. The water was 'bucketed' out of a small lake from which a pretty little stream flowed. There were yellow irises on the banks and a marshy meadow full of golden king-cups. My mother had to drive about four miles to get drinking water from a spring.

There were two carriers' vans that went from Stokenchurch to Wycombe daily. They were affectionately called the 'Bluebird' and the 'Tin Lizzie'; they carried passengers and goods. When we went to London we walked one and a half miles to Kingston Crossing, which was just a small hut by the level crossing; from there we caught the 'Watlington Donkey', just two carriages, to Risborough and from there to London. Quite an easy journey, really, as the trains connected every time.

By about 1920 the Oxford and Watlington buses were running into Wycombe four times a day, thus opening a new world for people living in isolated places.

Although the farmworkers' wages were very low and there were no luxuries, they had many privileges and were not short of food and warmth. There were plenty of logs for the open fires and the oil lamps provided background warmth as well as a gentle light. The cottage gardens were large and they grew plenty of fruit and vegetables. The main crop potatoes and swedes were grown in the fields. The farmworker had free milk and kept pigs and poultry to provide meat and eggs.

Hill Farm is now part of a larger farming unit about five times the original size. With modern methods and machinery it is efficiently farmed by the same number of men that my father employed nearly sixty years ago.

M. Smith, *Bledlow Ridge*

As a child I lived in Studley Green on the main London to Oxford Road, about six miles west of High Wycombe. The roads were made of flint, and were dusty and full of pot holes. Women wearing large sacking aprons used to go into the fields stone picking for a few pence. These stones were collected up and put into large heaps by the roadside and were then used for filling the holes and were rolled in by a steamroller. Traffic at that time was mostly horse drawn.

Studley Green

Flint picking

103

When the beech trees were felled in the woods, the tops were cut off and sold to local people for firewood. Then heavy chains were fixed round the logs and teams of horses dragged these through the woods to waiting timber wagons. They were then taken to the sawmills to be cut up into planks ready for chairmaking. I have stood and watched chair legs being made locally with the old pole lathe. We could buy a large bag of wood chips or shavings for a few pence. The chair legs were taken to High Wycombe or Stokenchurch by horse and cart to be put with other parts and made into chairs, some with solid seats, some cane or rush matting seats done by local women in their own homes. The main industry of High Wycombe and district was chairmaking and the town at one time was noted for chairs, chapels and children.

All the houses in the district were lit by oil lamps. Sanitation was very primitive, usually in a little wooden hut down the garden or in an outhouse.

Water for all purposes came from rain water tanks in the garden, pumped up with a hand pump near the sink. One year was a very dry summer and the tanks ran dry. We flocked down to a well in the woods and drew up lovely spring water—men and women with buckets slung from a wooden yoke round their shoulders, slats of wood called 'swimmers' were placed on top of the water in the buckets to avoid spillage. We had a long walk to get to the well, down a stony road called the 'pitch' to Beacons Bottom, a hamlet in the valley, then across meadows into Bottom Wood. The hamlet of Beacons Bottom lies in the valley a quarter of a mile down a side road, past the Harrow and rows of old cottages. In the summer, two local women sat at their door, making Bucks pillow lace. I used to watch their nimble fingers moving the bobbins. At the far end was a low thatch-roofed workshop where chair legs were turned with the pole lathe. At one time, there was a

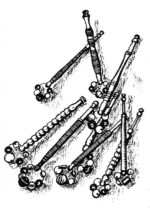

Lace-making
bobbins

public house, the local school, and a flint and slate-roofed Methodist chapel. I attended both as a child.

When the new Dashwood Hill was made, the roads were tarmaced over as cars were becoming more numerous. The most popular at that time were the old bull-nosed Morris Cowley cars, 'T' Fords, Swift two-seaters and later Austin Sevens.

These are some of my childhood memories, when we were content with simple pleasures and very happy.

Winifred D. Newell, *Sands*

My father was a Windsor frame maker and we lived in Crown Court, West Wycombe. There were seven girls and one boy in my family and my mother kept a little shop just down the lane selling sweets, cigarettes and soft drinks, to help out. In summer we hired out sledges and also boiled water for picnic teas. Sledging down West Wycombe Hill is a summer sport. The grass is grazed very short by rabbits and the sledges are the backs of Windsor chairs with slats fastened across them and made slippery with linseed oil.

West Wycombe

My mother had to pay twopence a week per child for our schooling, which amounted to quite a large sum in those days. As soon as I had passed my exams I left school and went to work at G. North & Sons as a rush and fancy straw worker. I was eleven years old and worked there until I married at twenty-one.

I remember having nightmares for a week when they took up the floor boards in our cottage and found the skeleton of a man under there. We never did find out how long he'd been there or who he was.

I once saw a man who had hung himself in Brench

Wood. We young ones got there just as they cut him down and he rolled down the hill, his dinner bag still on his back. Some men got a sheep hurdle to put him on, dinner bag and all. His name was J.B. Spencer.

As a child, I remember the village crier calling 'Hay-O, Hay-O' and then telling the news. We used to watch the coach and horses draw up at the George and Dragon, and always went down there to watch the Hunt start, the men in their red coats and the packs of hounds milling around the horses' feet.

I used to attend the sewing classes at The House (West Wycombe Park) run by the then Lady Dashwood. We learned pillow lace, principally.

Mr Coles, Mr Rippington and Mr Spicer used to play the handbells throughout the village at Christmas. Mr Hughes, the milkman, called every morning with his can of milk and measured out what each household wanted. At Christmas he used to give my mother a Christmas stocking full of sugar watches or sugar sausages for us children.

Of course, there were May Revels too.

There was very little traffic in those days. We girls used to string our skipping rope right across the Oxford Road. At the outbreak of the Boer War we marched abreast right into High Wycombe to see the boys off—right down the middle of the Oxford Road. That October day in 1899 was bitter cold.

My Uncle Tom from Turville was a chair bodger and worked mostly in the woods. The only time he went as far as Wycombe, it was foggy and he saw nothing at all.

I remember my Aunt Eliza calling 'Little girl, little girl, I want you. Go fetch me a pint of porter and a pottle of potatoes'. A pottle measure holds about two pounds.

A bodger's shop.

Kate Brookes, *Sands*

VII
Newport
Hundred

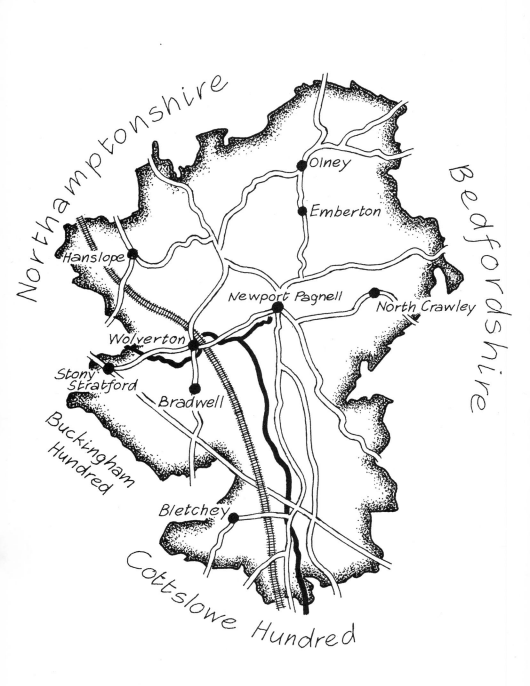

Northamptonshire

Bedfordshire

Olney

Emberton

Hanslope

Newport Pagnell

North Crawley

Wolverton

Stony
Stratford

Bradwell

Buckingham
Hundred

Bletchey

Cottslowe Hundred

By far the best known family in Bletchley when we were young was the Leon family.

Herbert Samuel Leon came from Hamburg where he was a banker. He bought a farm not far from the railway station and gradually built it up into a fine estate of several hundred acres. It was called Bletchley Park and the farmstead was replaced by a magnificent mansion. This still stands and houses the Post Office Training School. The size of the place can be judged by the fact that he employed two hundred men, forty of whom were gardeners. Eight men were employed solely in attending the two orchid houses, two men being always 'on the wheel' which meant that two men were on duty all night all the year round to ensure the exact temperatures being maintained. I know this is correct because I was once courted by one of these young men.

Mr Leon stood for Parliament as a Liberal and for many years represented this constituency. For his services he was knighted and dropped his familiar name of Sammy to become Sir Herbert Leon. With Lady Leon he did a great deal of social work in Bletchley, visiting the sick and needy, donating playing fields and recreation grounds, housing their employees and generally looking after their welfare.

One year there was a huge Liberal demonstration at Bletchley Park with speakers of national repute, sports of all kinds, horse-jumping and fireworks. This was the forerunner of the Bletchley August Show on Bank Holiday Monday which became nationally famous. Special trains were run and people came in by foot, bicycle, pony trap and on horseback. My uncle came from Shrewsbury every year to join forces with my father in showing fruit and vegetables of all kinds, for which they gained many prizes. There were a tennis tournament, flower show, sheep-dog trials, horse-jumping, a fun-fair, athletics of all kinds, tugs-of-war, cycling, floodlit dancing, a brass band playing throughout the day and finally a gigantic firework display.

There were two main entrances to the Park, both guarded by lodges. The lower drive wound around the grounds, passed the sports pavilion, cricket pitch and tennis courts and coppices before joining the main drive. Sometimes one could see through the wrought-iron gates in the distance in front of the mansion, a landau driven by a coachman in a top hat and drawn by magnificent horses, bearing inside a dignified handsome couple, Sir Herbert and Lady Leon.

One thing Sir Herbert hated was the sound of the church bells. He tried many times to get the ringing stopped but the rector, a strong character, formidable even to those of his flock who absented themselves from church, was adamant: the church had been there over seven hundred years before Sir Herbert. Only as he lay on his death bed did the rector grant him his request.

My father was shepherd and butcher to Sir Herbert and I had a happy childhood on this estate. Now all that is recognizable from the old days is the mansion itself, the lake in front of it, the sports pavilion now used as a Music Centre and the upper lodge. Everything else has gone.

Amy Constance Knill, Ethel Houldridge and Eliza Gladwin,
Old Bletchley

In 1884 I started school. I had to take twopence a week while I was in the infants' room and fourpence a week when older.

There were only two rooms, one for the infants and one for the rest where two teachers taught at the same time.

In the infants' room we sat on a gallery—a tiered platform—the new children on the bottom tier, the others sitting higher up, according to their age. When you reached the highest tier of the gallery you were ready to go into the big room.

Amy Constance Knill

On very cold, frosty, winter mornings, instead of being allowed to stay in the classroom at playtimes we had to put on our outdoor clothes, line up in the playground, take hold of the coat-tail of the child in front and run as far as the thatched cottage at the end of the road and back, a distance of about half a mile. We were thus warmed up for the next lesson.

Eliza Gladwin

My memories of starting school in 1908 are happy ones.

The very first day in the 'babies' class we were given nine pieces of different coloured wools. By means of these we were taught numbers as well as colours. Even small sums were done with these pieces. If we were good and worked well we had a ride on the rocking horse.

In the next class we began to learn the alphabet using charts and the teacher's blackboard. We each had a tray of silver sand and a pointer, something like a butcher's wooden skewer. With these we laboured to write, first letters then words. This was a good idea because if we did something wrong, we just shook the tray and began again.

Louisa Shouler, *Old Bletchley*

Spelling tray for infants

I am 97 years old but I remember vividly my grandfather refusing to leave the Old Swan which he had kept for sixty years. The thatched roof was being pulled down about him before he was finally persuaded to quit. He had never had a case in court the whole time he'd been there. He was a gentle man, whilst my grandmother was a fierce woman, quite able to carry on while my grandfather was away for days at a time with his drill sowing the farmers' seeds.

During Bletchley Feast the Swan was open day and night and though the fairground people were often rowdy, my grandparents were always able to cope.

Railway men coming off the night shift would call for a drink before going home to breakfast. Often my grandfather was still trying, at 2 pm, to persuade them to go home to sleep for a few hours before their next turn of duty. There were no set opening hours in those days. Whenever someone demanded drink or food it had to be served.

112

The Swan was pulled down and a red brick monstrosity erected in its place.

The rival public house, a wattle and daub thatched cottage, the Shoulder of Mutton, was situated at the village crossroads and managed to survive until ten years ago. This house being on the main highway from Buckingham to Fenny Stratford had more casual travellers than the Swan which was set back round the corner from the crossroads.

Eliza Gladwin

Aylesbury ducks

Bletchley always had an abundance of water. Almost every field had its pond, every cottage its well and the presence of springs could be detected by the streams of water ever running out of banks. This plentiful supply often caused severe flooding in the rainy season. One man's death is partly attributable to excess of water. Being a farmer, he went to market once a week at Fenny Stratford by pony and trap. One particularly wet and stormy night the pony took the last bend in the road at the bottom of a long steady hill too sharply. The trap tipped over, throwing its occupant into the full ditch. By the time he was found, he was drowned. Ever since the spot has been known as 'Mobb's corner'.

Duck Lane was always flooded regularly as it was

113

in the lowest lying part of the village. As the name suggests ducks were to be found on the pond there. School Lane also boasted a pond on which the scholars used to skate and slide on their way to school. High hedges along this narrow lane made ideal courting territory.

Church Lane was the only other road in the parish apart from the narrow road which led out of the village at the cross roads to Newton Longville and another to Shenley.

The hedgerows were alive with bird life, small mammals and insects of every kind. The verges contained every species of wild flower imaginable. Today—hundreds and hundreds of council estate houses! No yellowhammers flitting about, no nightingales filling the air with sweetness.

Ivy Fisher, Amy Constance Knill and Laura May Morris,
Old Bletchley

Bletchley Station has always been of great importance since it was constructed. It was the junction for the Oxford and Cambridge branch lines as well as being the main through line from Euston to Scotland. This was not always so for at one time it was the end of the line. Passengers had to alight at Denbigh bridge just beyond the station, board the stage coach at the Denbigh Inn and proceed along Watling Street to the next railway station—Rugby. There is a plaque on the side of the bridge to commemorate this phemomenon.

The actual approach to the station covered a large area, with livery stables at one side nearest the main road. Huge horses were used to shunt trucks and carriages about, as almost all goods were transported by rail, and the horses used for drawing the wagons were also kept here. One could hire a horse and carriage from these stables, too. Bricks from Newton Longville were brought by horse and cart and stacked into trucks standing in the sidings at the goods yard.

Bletchley, being in the heart of the Whaddon Chase Hunt country, was the station to which hunters and horses travelled. Two huge mounting blocks stood at the main entrance to the station and were there until the recent electrification of the line and structural alteration of the station approach. Stabling on a large scale was provided by Deacon's stables opposite the station. Horses were left here for the season and tended by resident grooms. This system remained in operation until the 1914-18 war when the stables were requisitioned as a timber supply yard and manned by prisoners of war.

Sir Herbert Leon had a horse trough erected at the entrance to the station approach and it was there for many years after horses had disappeared from the general scene.

Ivy Fisher and Gertrude Collins, *Old Bletchley*

Bletchley Feast was always held on the first Saturday after the seventh of September. The village came alive for this very important social occasion for everyone went for the fun.

It was held on the village green, Three Tree Square as it was called because of the three large elms which grew there. Stalls of all kinds were put up around the green while the funfair had the centre site. The stall I liked best was the brandy snap stall—never were such delicious brandy snaps!

Amy Constance Knill

115

One of the highlights of our childhood was when the hunters and hounds met at Three Tree Square. Around the green small thatched cottages stood, a public house called the Shoulder of Mutton and a farm known as Manor Farm.

The pink coats, white breeches of the men, the long black side-saddle skirts of the women, the highly polished boots, the shiny top hats, the well-groomed beautiful horses, the friendly but eager-to-be-away hounds, all made a never-to-be forgotten picture. Everyone who possibly could followed as long as they were able, on foot or on bicycles.

My brothers ran miles, opening and shutting gates to earn some money.

Ethel Houldridge

Sunday really was a day of rest and worship. No work was done except the bare essentials. Every member of the household went to church and chapel at least once a day and some went three times.

A certain amount of slackness was creeping into this strict custom by the time I was old enough to be taken to church, possibly because the First World War was drawing to its conclusion and many things never returned to what they had been before 1914. My grandmother used to relate how the rector would be sure to visit during the week any member of his flock who had failed to appear at church on Sunday—and woe betide him or her if no valid excuse was forthcoming. There was no backsliding in his day.

He was able to keep this paternal eye upon his children because Bletchley was a small village of one hundred houses until about sixty-five to seventy years ago. So the rector's task of knowing everyone would not have been difficult.

Ivy Fisher

My father came to Bletchley to be cowman to Lord Dalmeny, now Lord Rosebery, who was then living at the Grange. After years of hard work, one day Lord Dalmeny accused my father of not looking after the cows properly and said that the quality of the milk was very much below standard. My father was a very conscientious worker and this riled him so much that he said he'd leave as he wasn't giving satisfaction. Of course, we had to come out of the farm cottage and he got a job at the brickworks, digging clay for the bricks which were all hand made in those days. For this he was paid sixpence an hour.

Not long after he started this new job, Lord Dalmeny came and begged him to go back as cowman because he had found out that the cook was skimming the milk, making butter and sending it home to her relatives in Ireland. But my father refused, saying that if Lord Dalmeny could not take his word, then he was not the boss for him!!

Monica Savage, *Old Bletchley*

In 1880 there was only one tiny shop in the village. In fact it was really the front parlour of a thatched cottage used as a general store. Mrs Chandler looked after the customers while her husband was away doing his job as postman. Although Bletchley was such a small village at that time, this was a full time job for him because he had to walk to Whaddon and Newton Longville if there were mail for these places. Each is a good three miles distant in opposite directions from each other, and the only means of transport then was on foot. If fine and dry he could walk across the fields to Whaddon, thus shortening his journey by a mile.

The cobbler lived in Yew Tree Cottage in Church

Lane. As there was no shoe shop we had our shoes made for us—and we had to take good care of them.

In Duck Lane lived a candle-maker. His trade used to stink to high heaven. On Sundays he preached in the little chapel, next door to his cottage. It held twenty people.

A chimney sweep lived in the same row of cottages. He was nearly always drunk and one never knew whether he would turn up to sweep the chimney on the day arranged—or next day, or a week after. He worked in his spare time as odd job man at the two public houses.

Amy Constance Knill, Gertrude Collins and George Chandler (member's husband and son of founder member) *Old Bletchley*

My father, John Meager, and my grandfather and great-grandfather all followed a trade which has completely disappeared—that of wheelwright. Even before my father's early death in 1936 things were changing drastically and he was fast becoming a builder of houses instead of farm carts and implements.

But I can remember quite clearly the lay-out of all the buildings. The massive barn with its great timbered beams was the wheelwright's shop. All along one side were windows underneath which were the wheelwrights' benches; racks of tools at eye-level above the benches were kept in perfect order, everything in its proper place. Each man had his own tools, and no-one dared to touch them. Across the shop was the turning lathe with its deep pit beneath for shavings.

A door out of this barn led into a long dark shed which housed the timber, great long planks of various woods, and this in turn led into another barn which had a loft above where hay was kept for the horses beneath.

118

At the top end of the wheelwright's shop another door led into the blacksmith's shop. The floor of the working end was cobbled but the end where the horses were tethered to be shod was made of long, well-worn wooden planks.

Besides horse-shoes the blacksmith had to make tyres for the wheels made in the main shop. When a wheel was ready for its tyre six or seven men were pressed into action to 'shut' the tyre into place. Great speed and skill was needed for this vital operation for tyres had to fit and not be liable to 'open'.

Besides these larger things, the blacksmith could make small objects such as door-hinges, window fasteners and gate catches; and besides wheels and carts, the wheelwrights made barrows, gates, candle-sticks, stools, tables, cupboards, wooden toys, in fact almost anything that was made of wood. When completed all these things were transferred to the paint shops.

Beyond all these buildings stretched the fields and the main orchard with its massive walnut tree which gave its name to the new house, built in 1919, Walnut Tree Cottage.

The skills which were in such great demand a hundred years ago and for which the 'Meagers' were famed, have been lost along the road of progress.

Ivy Fisher

Bradwell

The village of Bradwell has not changed much in the last thirty years, but that will soon be altered when Milton Keynes gets busy.

Once we had a vicar for the Parish of Bradwell but now he has to look after Loughton and Shenley as well as Bradwell.

There were three public houses but one was closed a few years ago. The village school was filled with over forty children, but about ten years back the number was only eight, so it was closed and the children are taken by coach to New Bradwell. The school is now a very nice house.

There used to be three shops in the village. There is only one now, but luckily it is a post office so we don't have to go far for our pensions.

Our three farm houses are all empty and the land left vacant.

Evelyn Haseldine, *Bradwell*

How we looked forward to and enjoyed Shrove Tuesday, a half-holiday from school when we all went paper chasing over the fields. Being a church school we had another day's holiday next day, Ash Wednesday. To make sure of a good mark on school register we went to church, but the rest of the day was ours to do as we liked. The next big event in our lives was Whitsuntide, and big athletic sports took place on the Monday. The next highlight of our childhood was the annual pageant. Planning and rehearsing went on for months and every year had a different theme. We had little money and all our fun had to be made by ourselves.

Kathleen Shirley, *Bradwell*

A very eventful day in our lives was the Sunday School treat and several times we went for it on a barge. We boarded the boat by the bridge up the Old Bradwell road and off the poor horse would start until we got to Great Linford. When we got to our

Nearing Great Linford

destination, Fenny Stratford, we all disembarked and went into a large field where we ran races, scrambled for sweets and had our tea. Coming back at dusk the men of the party got out and helped pull the rope so that the horse would have it a little easier.

In the winter children learned scripture for a Lord Wharton bible. This gentleman had left money in his will for these bibles for the children who could say passages of scripture by heart.

On Sunday evenings in the spring and summer we went for long walks, sometimes up the fields to Linford Wood where Milton Keynes City Centre is to be, or along the canal and down by Stanton Lane to St Peter's Church, which the Lord Bishop of Oxford has just declared redundant, and then on through the fields to Haversham Mill. I used to wonder where the underground passage was which rumour said ran from the church to Bradwell Abbey. Other times we walked along the towpath to Great Linford past the limestone quarries where parents took children who had whooping cough as it was good for them.

On an Easter Monday my parents sometimes took us to Stony Stratford to watch all the traffic coming back from Towcester Races. This was exciting for us as we never saw so much traffic the rest of the year. Most of it was horse-drawn vehicles.

On a Sunday morning the local baker used to cook the meat and Yorkshire pudding. My mother made her Yorkshire and put it in her tin, then put her meat on a stand and took it to the bake-house. There the baker gave her a metal disc with a number on it and put an identical one on the meat. At one o'clock she went back, and as he pulled them out of the oven he called the numbers out, and my mother would then claim our dinner and hurry home.

When we went to my grandmother's to stay in winter she always warmed our beds with a warming pan. It frightened me when she took the red hot embers from the fire and put them in the pan.

We had a cycling club at school and one of the teachers used to take us to places of interest such as Olney where the poet Cowper once lived. Now the Pancake Race is run there between America and England. Brickhill Woods and Woburn Park, not then open to the public, were among our favourite rides.

E.M. Toddy, *Bradwell*

Emberton

Emberton is a small village situated in the north of the county, one and a half miles from Olney, with a square Clock Tower standing in the centre, in which a bell was tolled to call to the men working in the fields.

There was until recently a blacksmith's forge—always very busy shoeing horses for hunting, working on farms and drawing traps. A four-wheeled 'fly', driven by Arther Brown, met all trains arriving at Olney Station—now closed.

Cattle were taken on foot by drovers to markets at Bedford, Northampton and Wellingborough, and any cattle found straying were put into 'the pound', a field attached to Manor Farm, until claimed, a small charge being made.

Near the forge was the village pump where women filled their buckets for a day's supply. It was never known to go dry.

122

A horse show was held annually on Bank holiday in one of the farm's fields.

At Emberton Feast and other holiday occasions Morris Dancers danced around the Tower—afterwards taking refreshment at the Bell or the Bear Inn (now gone). Sports were held for children and grown-ups and a meat tea was provided in the Dutch barn. School children danced round the maypole.

In the winter a Plum Pudding Party was held in the village schoolroom—when plum puddings boiled in many of the surrounding cottages were served—everyone holding a hot plate in readiness.

On Sundays people carried their dinner to be cooked at the village bakehouse, the meat in a baking tin covered with a cloth and Yorkshire pudding batter in a jug or can, and at 'drawing time' would be seen hurrying home with it all ready to eat.

Across the River Ouse is Weston Underwood where the poet Cowper sat in his summer-house in The Wilderness writing his poems and where in the spring is to be seen a carpet of snowdrops.

A. Fairey, *Emberton*

Cowper's Summer House as at turn of century

Emberton where I was born in 1892 has always seemed a happy, friendly village, partly owing to the lasting influence of my grandparents, parents and cousin who lived and served in the Old Rectory for nearly a hundred years. My parents regularly visited every house and cottage, my mother with the shawl which she knitted for each new baby, while my father had his sticky pockets stuffed with almond toffee and peppermints for the children.

We always kept huge dogs, Great Danes and Russian Wolfhounds.

Our front gate was always open and the villagers

allowed to walk through the garden and use our field for picnics.

The lovely church was nearly always full, extra chairs being needed for Christmas and Harvest festivals, and the six bellringers and our churchyard were the pride of the countryside. Most of the stained-glass windows were put in to the memory of my grandparents and uncles; Grandmamma's is dedicated to 'Faith, Hope and Charity'. Poor thing, she must have needed all three with thirteen children on £250 a year, but they all grew up hale and hearty.

Seventy years ago in Emberton the roads were terrible, covered with small stones and needing the constant use of steamrollers which terrified our horses.

The climate was quite different. For months there was hot sunshine and all meals were taken at a long table under the big plane trees, but the winters were bitter and we skated for days on the river and flooded fields between Weston and the Olney road.

We made our own pleasure, and as the families varied from seven of us to thirteen children at both Filgrave and Clifton rectories, it was easy to collect two teams for hockey and cricket matches and every big house had its own tennis court. My elder sisters were renowned for arranging plays and concerts which meant three months' hard work, and one sister spent chilly hours in the cellar painting scenery. Twice a week twenty lucky children came to learn choruses for flowers and fairies and were quite contented with two sweets at the end.

We also taught country dancing and took parties of boys and girls to Tyringham and Gayhurst in fancy dress.

One of our plays was *A Pageant of the Queens*, acted by twenty WI members, beginning with the poisoning of Queen Boadicea and ending with the Queen Mother. No one was anxious to be Bloody Mary so I borrowed a ruby velvet frock and leapt delightedly into my three-minute scene set to music in which I was signing a Death Warrant. My brother wrote an appropriate verse for each Queen which we sent to Buckingham Palace and in three days we had a charming letter from Lady Delia Peel, telling us that the Queen Mother had thoroughly enjoyed reading them.

We could usually count on at least four dances at Christmas at Tyringham, Crawley Grange and Gayhurst and the satin or silk long dresses, sometimes sparkling with silver sequins, low necks—but not *too* low—and white kid gloves to the shoulders were so very pretty. We had pale pink or blue programmes with pencils danging on matching silk to write in partners' names, but to have the same partner more than three times was considered highly improper. The sequined, handpainted and feathered fans were enchanting, and there was great variety in the dances: waltzes, polkas, Washington Post, Pas de Quatres and the Lancers in which one was invariably swung off ·one's feet.

The river too was a great joy, as we had a large boat called the 'Old Aunt Jane' in which we rowed up to an island near Filgrave and built a fire to boil the kettle. I dreaded going under Olney bridge towards the mill because the great wheel threatened to drag us down and grind us to bits.

Sidney Sams, *Emberton*

I was born in Hanslope and I remember so well the growing of corn by all the allotment holders. My father worked in the Railway Works at Wolverton. About the month of August when the corn was ready, he used to have to go straight from work to

the allotments where my two sisters and I met him
with his tea so that he could start right away to cut
the corn with a sickle. This was a slow job, and we
children used to have to help tie up the corn. But the
event that pleased us was when the corn was thrashed
on a Saturday with the old thrashing engine. All the
children gathered in the field and we had an exciting
day with all our fathers, finishing the day with their
own sacks of corn.

As my father worked in the Railway Works he had
a railway pass, so we could afford to visit relatives in
Derbyshire. But the exciting start to the holiday was
riding to Castlethorpe station in an open landau,
hired from a man in the village.

Emily Mary Reeves, *Hanslope*

'If Hanslope Spire was ten time higher, I would take
off my shoe and hop over it.'

This was very confusing until it was explained to
me.

E.M. Toddy, *Bradwell*

I remember the celebrations that took place on
Empire Day, 24 May, at school. After the calling of
the register we assembled in the playground where
the Union Jack was hoisted. We then had a good sing-
song of patriotic songs such as 'British Grenadiers',
'Hearts of Oak', 'Rule Britannia', 'God Bless the
Prince of Wales'.

Lessons would continue. After dinner we went to
school dressed in our second-best clothes. The school
choir gave a special recital and we had country

dancing. The high light of the day was the presentation of the Empire Day medals.

A 'Nobility' of the village was asked to make the presentations and these medals were given to the boys and girls who had come top in their classroom exams. These medals were made of what looked like aluminium, slotted at the top to hold a ribbon of red, white and blue colour. For Class 6 there was a bronze medal.

Children who had won medals in previous years wore them with great pride.

Evelyn Cadwell, *Hanslope*

North Crawley

The population of the village is now just under five hundred with twenty-six children in the school. In 1895 there were one hundred and twenty children in the school, with three families of twelve children each.

Children were allowed to leave at eleven if they had a 'Dunce's Certificate'. The school had galleried seating with long desks.

In 1895 the migration from farm working started and men went to the Railway Works at Wolverton.

Crawley Grange employed a number of village folk, and had a coachman and groom with cockades in their hats. Their first car was a yellow Packard in 1904.

It is a debatable point where the villagers were buried as the churchyard does not have any very old graves, or very few. It is thought that old graves are under the square in front of the church, known as the Waste Ground, and indeed human remains have been found when digging. This square was used as a

127

pound for men driving cattle or sheep to and from markets.

Crawley Feast was held on the Waste Ground on the Monday nearest 12 October. Fair men paid their dues to be there two days, and when one year they failed to pay the dues the Fair discontinued. Lovely pink spiced pears were sold for a halfpenny each. They were baked locally and carried to the Fair in big earthenware dishes. On the Monday evening a dance was organised to raise funds for the Sewing Girls' Picnic.

There were three bakehouses in the village, showing that bread formed an important part of the daily food. There were four public houses and a beerhouse which was a tavern where the men could lodge over night when driving animals. A butcher came every Saturday and there was a butcher's shop. There were three brickfields and there are still cottages standing built from their beautiful red rosy bricks. Some were said to be built from the discards, but are still beautiful.

On Whit Monday the village band went to Crawley Grange to fetch Dr Boswell, marched up the village street to fetch the rector and then to church, subsequently playing for country dancing for the Women's Club.

In 1881 a census was taken and showed nine hundred and ninety nine inhabitants. The thousandth was the rector who was courting in a neighbouring village!

Laundry was taken from Crawley Grange to Newport Pagnell in a horse-brake drawn by a roan mare. If there was room, passengers were taken at the cost of 2d. On Wednesdays and Saturdays if the villagers walked three miles to Cranfield, they could get a horse brake to Bedford for one shilling. For special occasions to meet visitors a horse and cart could be hired for half-a-crown.

Butter was a luxury because of the shortage of winter feed.

Mrs Maslin herself went to the Wolverton Centre as a pupil teacher. She walked four miles to Newport Pagnell Station to catch the local train, known as 'Nobby Newport', to Wolverton. At the end of the day she returned by train to Newport Pagnell and then walked four miles home. This was in 1904.

Henrietta Maslin (born 1890), *North Crawley*

River Ouse
near Stony Stratford

When I was a child Blind Barley, his dog and his concertina, were a familiar sight in our little town. He was a tall, spare, white-haired old man. He never came out until dusk when, led by his dog, he began his evening round, stopping at street corners to play a hymn from his repertoire. Some of the tunes were sad, others were lively rollicking Salvation Army ones. Occasionally he uttered a fervent 'Alleluia', or 'Praise the Lord'.

Stony Stratford

When the evening was still and star-lit you could hear him from a long way off, even the gay tunes sounding melancholy in the cold night air. When or where he died I do not know but the memory of his gentleness, piety and patience has stayed with me to this day.

Mrs Elstone lived in our little town at the corner where the Horsefair Green joins Silver Street.

In one of her windows stood a glass-topped case in which were displayed a fascinating collection of bone and wooden bobbins, lace collars, cuffs, borders and edgings of gossamer fineness and a necklace of many-coloured beads. These beads of soft blue, gold and yellow, delicately ornamented with tiny flowers had been used to weight the bobbins on the lace pillow, for Mrs Elstone dealt with Buckinghamshire pillow lace.

She was perhaps one of the last remaining lace buyers in the district, for by the 1920's lacemaking as a cottage industry had practically died out.

In the early 1900's when life was uneventful, one of the most eagerly awaited events of the year was Stratford Fair.

It arrived at the beginning of our summer holidays, and for days beforehand we strained our eyes for the first glimpse of the traction engine with its gleaming barley-sugar-stick columns of brass that headed the procession.

Of the van dwellers, the one I remember best is the shooting gallery lady. She always drove her own van, sitting proudly erect in the front, her strong brown hands loaded with gold rings. Her dress was a tight black bodice and long black skirt, while on her pile of grey hair she wore a fine big hat of black velvet, lavishly adorned with feathers. Her profile was aristocratic, her cheeks tanned and deeply wrinkled. From her ears hung long gold peardrops that swung rhythmically with every movement of the wagon.

When I first remember Stratford Fair it stood on the Market Square, overflowing into Silver Street and on to the Horsefair Green.

The steam organ was an impressive sight. Made in Brussels, it sported little painted plaster boys and girls, staring woodenly ahead as they tapped their drums and triangles.

'George Billings and Sons. Famous Galloping Horses. Patronised by Royalty and all the Leading Gentry and Nobility'. Mr Billings was a short, plump, rubicund man. I never saw him without his bowler hat.

Between the wars the Fair was transferred to a

field in the Wolverton Road and there it continued until the shadow of Milton Keynes fell upon North Buckinghamshire. Then the field was scheduled for building and people now live where once the Fair stood.

Mabel Coleman, *Mursley*

I was born in 1894 in Wolverton where I lived until 1942.

Wolverton

When three years old I started school in Wolverton Infants' School. This school was then in the building which is now the Market Hall. The playground is now occupied by the Church Institute.

Very soon we were all celebrating the Diamond Jubilee of Queen Victoria and a gentleman gave all the children in the Infants' School a silver threepenny piece.

The first moving picture I ever saw was of the funeral procession of Queen Victoria. It was shown at the August Fair at Stony Stratford.

Mabel Brown, *Bradwell*

In Wolverton, just before the First World War, carol singers still used to come round early on May Day morning. Small groups of children, carrying a May garland and a collecting box, called at the houses and sang,

'A bunch of May I have brought you
And at your door it stands
It's well set out and well spread about
By the work of our Lord's hands.'

131

The garland was often a small hoop, covered with coloured tissue paper and flowers but sometimes the carol singers pushed a decorated wooden pushchair. Even the baby in it was covered in daisy chains!

The flowers used were often cowslips and bluebells. The bunch of May was usually only in bud, as on this cold clay soil it was hardly ever in flower by 1 May.

M.G. Knight, *Dunsmore*

VIII
Stoke
Hundred

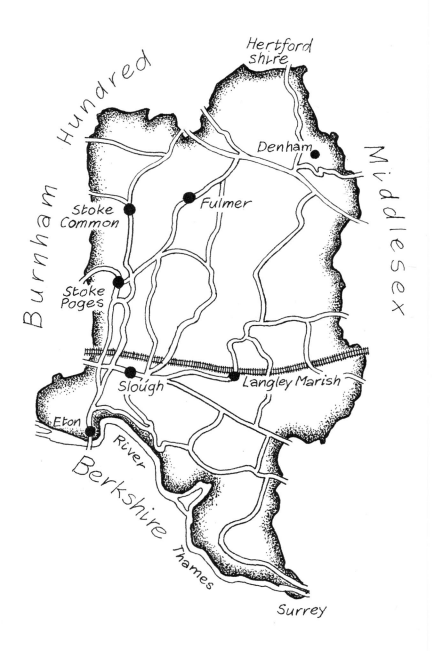

Hertford shire

Denham

Burnham Hundred

Middlesex

Stoke Common

Fulmer

Stoke Poges

Slough

Langley Marish

Eton

River

Berkshire

Thames

Surrey

I was born in Langley, Bucks, in March 1924 and have lived in Bucks the best part of my life. We used to walk through fields and over the farm land which stretched for miles around and wander along the stream running into Datchet. Over the last few years many houses and new housing estates have been built and all farms and fields done away with. In the village there was a blacksmith in a tiny row of houses, now turned into a block of modern houses, and also a home-made bakery which was there for years. It was run by Mr and Mrs Rymes and family. They are quite old now.

Nearby was a quaint cottage and some old-fash-ioned public houses, one called the Plough. Also in the village were a sweet shop, food shop and a greengrocer which have now been furnished with more modern fronts. The old police station has been done away with and a modern one put up in the main High Street. On the whole the village of Langley has become more than a village and some of the Langley residents who have lived there all their lives have seen many changes. We have a Free Church in the village and also a really old church, called St Mary's. On the Langley Road, there was a big childrens' orphanage which has now been demolished. Nearby was the Research Station. The cobbler is still there, the business passed on to son from father.

In the village stood a very big house and estate belonging to the late Mr and Mrs Hillier, and every year there was a big fete and sports in the grounds. It has been made into a big convent, with very high walls around.

Now we have a big oil depot at Langley station. The big Hawker airfield has been turned into a Ford's motor factory and recently the new Hotel Inn has gone up on what used to be farm land. On the whole we are now a very modern village with six foster homes on the LCC estate, three in Blandford Road and three in Langley High Street run by the Hammersmith Borough. In each home are seven children of different age groups up to eighteen years old. We have many big modern schools and the area is really built up. But we still have a good many old Langley residents and a few familiar things left in our village.

M.W. Holding, *Langley Marish*

Stoke Common

Gerrards Cross was a very small village, and consisted mainly of the houses surrounding the common. The village shop, owned by Mr Wood, was adjacent to the French Horn public house and Mr Wood was also the baker. His daughter, Mrs Newman, with her husband opened a baker's shop near Gerrards Cross station after the railway was constructed from London to the Midlands.

The village school still stands, close to the Packhorse public house, and the Bull on the western end of the common was the stopping place for the four-in-hand coach which ran from London to Oxford.

Jesse Dell, a carrier, made the journey from Chalfont to London three times a week, summer and winter and was frequently called on to take material from Finsbury Park to Chalfont House.

It was great fun crossing the water splash in Chalfont Village, which remained until the advent of the motor car.

Besides being a builder, Mr Knight of Stoke Common was a wheelwright and undertaker—there was always a coffin being made in the carpenter's shop and a blacksmith regularly employed fitting the iron rims to the wagon wheels and making the various brackets and fittings required for the construction of the farm wagons. There were also two pit-sawyers constantly sawing tree trunks into planks.

Oil lamps were in use until the electricity supply was brought to Stoke Common after the First World War.

Collum Green Road was originally called Parish Lane and then One Pin Lane. Hedgerley Park was owned by Mrs Stevenson, and her farm bailiff lived at Colly Hill Farm (now a house called Tara). We had to go there each morning to get the milk.

I forget the name of the owner of Fulmer Hall but well remember the tea and firework display given by the owner on the occasion when his son was released from prison for his part in the Jameson Raid on the Transvaal. It must have been about 1898.

The only transport at that time was provided by Mr Glenister who lived at Mount Pleasant, Hedgerley Dean. He had a horse and waggonette and made the journey from Hedgerley to Slough morning and afternoon in the summer and mornings in the winter. He was a fine-looking man, resembling Edward VII, and he used to announce his approach with a tune on his horn. He would undertake to deliver or collect parcels in Slough and make purchases if required.

After the First World War, a Mr Potter and a Mr Clark operated small motor buses between Stoke Common and Slough and gave a very efficient service. Eventually they were displaced by Premier Bus Co., then the GWR, and later by London Transport.

There was no shop at Stoke Common and the

137

nearest doctor lived at Farnham Common. The Fox and Pheasant public house had been there for half a century and its nearest neighbours were the Sefton Arms (now the Six Bells) and the One Pin.

We frequently walked to Burnham Beeches, which to us meant the Plain, where there was a wooden hut from which sweets and ginger beer could be obtained. Nearby was a donkey stand where one could have a ride for one penny.

The Fair visited Stoke Common every year in the late summer—it was quite an event.

Honor Gamble, *Stoke Poges & Wexham*

Stoke Poges

The school in School Lane was originally the school for the boys and the girls of Stoke Poges and Wexham. It was a Board School, built in the 1870's, and replaced the old school in Rogers Lane. It was three schools in one, an infants for all up to the age of seven, and for above that age two segregated schools for boys and girls.

Some children went to school when they were only three years old; many left at the age of ten and when they left school the girls usually went into service. There was nothing else for them to do. School was not free. The children each paid one penny a week. Corporal punishment was administered where and when necessary. One little girl was taken into the cloakroom and soundly spanked by teacher because she said she did not want to go to school. That little girl is now eighty-five years old and it is her most vivid recollection of her school days.

Empire Day was always celebrated with songs in the morning, with the Union Jack flying, and a holiday in the afternoon. May Day meant dancing

138

Creeper-clad Stoke Poges Church around end of 19ᵗʰ C

round the maypole in the playground. Some children carried a maypole to the houses saying 'First of May is Garland Day, Please remember the Maypole' hoping to collect pennies.

On Sundays they went to Sunday School. Before St Andrews Church was built, the Methodists met in a building in Rogers Lane near the present village hall. There are houses there now. The Sunday School outing was usually to Burnham Beeches. The children rode there in farm wagons and sometimes even in coal wagons. Food and drink were supplied.

Every year there was a Christmas party organised by the vicar and curate. It was held in the Parish Hall, formerly the old school in Rogers Lane, and there was the usual Christmas tree and small gifts. Bonfire night was always celebrated with a huge bonfire on the common opposite the Fox and Pheasant.

Village shops supplied most of the everyday requirements—butcher, baker and post office and the general store. There were three postal deliveries a day—and a cottage loaf cost 3½d. Some people fetched their milk direct from a farm. Others had it delivered—the milkmen having churns from which

139

they measured the quantity required with his long-handled measure.

There was no shortage of water in the village. It was drawn from wells or pumps. For those who had no other supply of drinking water, there was a pump opposite the present Junior School in Rogers Lane. One well had frogs in it but some wells were fresh spring water and always pure.

Most of the men in the village worked on the big estates. In winter, when the weather was too severe for outside building work, men collected sheets of ice from the ponds and lakes, using tongs, and stacked the sheets of ice in the ice wells belonging to the big houses, Stoke Court and Stoke Place.

There was a fair amount of poaching of pheasants, partridges and pigeons. The pub would pay fourpence a rabbit. The skins of rabbits were sold to the rag-and-bone man. Those who could catch sparrows, which were a pest, received threepence a dozen and the sparrows were made into pies.

The chimney sweep charged sixpence for an ordinary chimney: he had a boy to climb the large chimneys. There were twenty-one chimneys at Stoke Court.

Some of the old roads which still exist today have new names. Duffield Lane used to be called Back Road, Templewood Lane was Donkey Road, Chapel Lane was Watery Lane, Hockley Lane was Green Lane, Plough Lane was Cock Lane, Farthing Green Lane was Church Road. It is said that Shaggy Calf Road was so named because a headless shaggy calf ran up the road.

To commemorate the Golden Jubilee of Queen Victoria the Jubilee Oak was planted—some say by the Queen herself—at the corner of Church Road where it crosses Park Road. All the school children attended the ceremony and sang songs.

Members of *Stoke Poges & Wexham*